THE HINDĪ BIOGRAPHY OF DĀDŪ DAYĀL

THE HINDĪ BIOGRAPHY OF
DĀDŪ DAYĀL

Winand M. Callewaert

MOTILAL BANARSIDASS
Delhi Varanasi Patna
Bangalore Madras

First Edition: Delhi, 1988

MOTILAL BANARSIDASS
Bungalow Road, Jawahar Nagar, Delhi 110 007

Branches
Chowk, Varanasi 221001
Ashok Rajpath, Patna 800 004
24 Race Course Road, Bangalore 560 001
120 Royapettah High Road, Mylapore, Madras 600 004

Computer Print-outs: Kuleuven, Belgium

ISBN: 81-208-0490-2

PRINTED IN INDIA
BY JAINENDRA PRAKASH JAIN AT SHRI JAINENDRA PRESS, A-45 NARAINA INDUSTRIAL AREA, PHASE I, NEW DELHI 110 028 AND PUBLISHED BY NARENDRA PRAKASH JAIN FOR MOTILAL BANARSIDASS, DELHI 110 007.

To our son

Winod

Born in Jaipur

Preface

A place changes because you change. In the sixties, when I first went to Jaipur I found a hot town 'where a snake crawls through the sand and leaves no trace behind, like an ascetic passing through this world, *Rajab*'. Later it became an overcrowded, ever expanding place, with quiet corners full of manuscripts. It was my base for trips into Rājasthān, where you should love rough going if you love manuscripts. But the days and nights in buses and monasteries were very rewarding and they made the present edition possible. Rājasthān became part of my life, not just because I spent a good deal of time working on the documents copied there. It gave me friends and -when everything is said and published- that is the most rewarding and lasting result of my scholarly *līlā*.

This book owes a lot to the many people who helped me. Svāmī Mangaldās, at whose *samādhi* in Kucāman my eyes fill with tears; Svāmī Nārāyaṇdās, the prolific writer who spent his last years in Ajmer; the staff of the Dādū Mahāvidyālay and Svāmī Harirāmjī of Narainā; Mr. A.S. Das and Mr. G.N. Bahura, of the City Palace, Jaipur; Prof. H. Māheshvarī, of Jaipur and Dr. B.M. Jāvāliyā, of Udaipur; Mr. and Mrs. U.C. Jain who were extremely helpful when our son was born in Jaipur.
I would also like to thank Dr. Mukund Lath for his very valuable suggestions for the translation, P. Holden, of Canberra for her revision of the English and Bart Op de Beeck for his assistance in the production.
And

> let an editor give what there is,
> and let the commentator say
> what might be and what ought to be.

Contents

CHAPTER I

The Janma Līlā

"I am the devotee Gopāl, an ascetic and a Baniyā.
My true guru is Dādū, the merciful one.
It was my great good fortune that I found shelter with him.
I sang the praises of that greatest of saints" (16.28).

When Jan Gopāl sat down to write the *Life Story of Dādū Dayāl*, around 1620[1], he could not have imagined that his text would ever be reproduced by computer, 366 years later. The very idea of a critical edition probably never occurred to him: scribes were not supposed to make mistakes while copying; they certainly did not alter the text or add anything.
His *Life Story* as it is now found in the manuscripts is a gold-mine of sectarian interpolations and variants, illustrating the growing biases in the early group of Dādū's followers. Very soon[2] in the history of the *pantha* efforts were made to 'explain' Dādū's association with the low caste of *dhuniyā's* and with Muslims, or to emphasize his celibacy.
The *Life Story* is interesting for another reason: it uses literary devices which sound very familiar to a reader of the Christian gospels and hagiographies.

The critical edition of this earliest reference to Dādū's life was considered necessary, because we find in the Sukh Dayāl Dādū edition of 1947 no reference to any of "the seven manuscripts"[3] the editor states to have consulted, and no distinction between the texts of the earlier and the later versions.

Is this the first English translation?

In his *Memo. on Bhasha Literature*[4] Rev. John Traill wrote from Jaipur, in 1884:

"I must revise the translations of Dadu's Bani of 20,000 lines *and his life by Jangopal of 3,000 lines*, for lately I got a very old copy of

(1) Orr:1947 states: "The original Life Story may perhaps be dated somewhere between 1610 and 1620 and its final revision about 1720-1730" (p. 26 and 209).
I have no arguments from which to comment on this date, except that the 'final revision' means 'enlargement' and was made much earlier.

(2) One of the manuscripts with the enlarged text (Ms. B, Narainā) is dated 1654 AD.

(3) *Śrī Dādū Janma Līlā Parci, (samkṣipta ṭikā sahit)*, ed. by Sukh Dayāl Dādū, Advocate, Jaipur, 1947, pp.2-3.

(4) The six sheets of this typewritten document are available in the India Office Library, London, attached to the manuscript of the *Dādūvāṇī* (ref. No. B28).

the Bani. It was written 234 years ago (i.e. 1650 AD) and differs slightly from the text I used while translating".

We should remember that in his Memo. Traill gives an outline of the existing religious vernacular literature, in order to be given a grant from the Government to collect and copy manuscripts.
The manuscripts we used for the translation of the *Līlā have only about 850 lines* (see further). In consequence, we may presume that Traill knew only of the enlarged version of Jan Gopāl's story (ca. 1,600 lines) or he exaggerated in order to get a bigger grant. In fact, most figures indicating the amount of literature of each poet are exaggerated in his Memo. The *Dādūvāṇī* has about 7,500 lines.

The question remains: has Traill translated the *Līlā* into English?
Orr[5] remarks that Traill's further work was interrupted by his death in 1909. He was a Missionary of the Church of Scotland in Jaipur. These missionaries left Jaipur in 1976 and my enquiries about the Archives of the Church (now Church of North India) took me to Delhi, Bangalore, Bombay and Edinburgh (Church of Scotland and The National Library of Scotland). But no trail so far of Traill's translation.

Sectarian Sources of Dādū's life

During the past few decades some lengthy studies have been devoted to Dādūdayāl and the Dādūpanth[6]. When writing a biography of Dādū, authors often give a list of sources without apparently having consulted the works they mention, with the result that most literature on the subject now available is to a great extent merely the result of copying from earlier writers.
Often, a mass of details about Dādū is given without a clear distinction being made between early documents and later information arising from tradition. In most cases the composition of an original work was followed by a wave of sectarian historians who indulged in laudatory embellishments to the point of the most fanciful 'miracle-mongering'.

For most sectarian biographers[7], Jan Gopāl's *Dādū Janma Līlā* -the very first biography- has served as the basic source.

When trying to find the kernel of truth from which later Dādū traditions grew, it is necessary to consider the two following factors:
(a) the time-lag between the life of Dādū and the date of compilation of his biography, and
(b) the tendency of both oral and written traditions to conform to certain archetypes for the behaviour of Sants, telling us how they should have acted.

To give just one example, illustrating this last factor: even if it is not true that Dādū was invited by Akbar and went to see him in Fatehpur Sikri, it was fitting that such an incident be recorded, since many other Sants were said to have been invited by Akbar. Thus, an examination of the sources must consider not only their date of composition, but their sectarian assumptions as well.

(5) Orr:1947, p. 9.
(6) In Hindi: V. Śarmā, *Sant-kavi Dādū aur unkā panth* (New Delhi, 1969) and K.P. Simha, *Dādūpanth evam uske sāhitya kā samīkṣātmak adhyayan* (Vārāṇasi, 1971). In English: W.G. Orr, *A Sixteenth-century Indian Mystic*, London, 1947.
(7) A detailed list and short description of the sectarian commentaries after Jan Gopāl's account, are given in Callewaert:1978, p. 22ff.

The second (early?) source for Dādū's life is the *Sant gun sāgar* by Mādhav Dās, who may have been one of Dādū's disciples. Information about this work (two thousand verses, un-edited) was given to me for the first time in 1973, by Mr. Sukhdayal Dādū of Delhi, who attributed it to Mādhav Dās. According to him, the work was composed in 1604 AD, i.e. one year after Dādū's death. If this were true, then most of the fanciful details in the later *Dādū janma lilā* would have their origin in the *Sant gun sāgar*. However, P.H. Śarmā:of Jaipur has already expressed his doubts about the authenticity of this date[8]. The doubt was confirmed by the octogenarian Dādūpanthi *sādhu* Swāmi Nārāyan Dās of Ajmer, who wrote that many manuscripts of this work have now been found, but that none is dated before 1910 AD[9]. He refers briefly to the details about Dādū's life in the *Sant gun sāgar* which differ from Jan Gopāl's account and presumes that the work was written at the beginning of the twentieth century.
Orr also refers to the *Sant gun sāgar* when he writes: "A second Janmalilā (after Jan Gopāl's), on much the same lines, is ascribed to another of Dādū's disciples, Madhu Das. This too is probably a re-edited version of a genuinely early work. In its present form it can hardly be placed earlier than 1800"[10].
Considering the uncertain date of composition, however, I classify the information found in this biography as a recent, sectarian tradition.

A third early source is the *Bhaktamāl* by Jaggā, one of the first generation of Dādū's disciples. In verses 33-69, a description is given of Dādū and his disciples. The work was edited by A. Nāhaṭā in his edition of the Rāghav Dās *Bhaktamāl*[11]. Unlike both the early and later versions of Jan Gopāl's *Dādū Janma Lilā*, verse 34 in the present work already makes mention of Dādū's foster-father 'by the name of Lodi'. This seems to indicate that the change in the account about Dādū's origin was brought about at an early stage in the tradition.

Rajab's *Sarvāṅgi*, a fourth major source, contains an important variant reading concerning Dādū's *dhuniyā* origin. In the fourteenth verse of the *Granth sādh māhimā* chapter (coming after chapter 22, *Bhajan pratāp*), the texts of all the manuscripts used in my edition (except F and J) agree in writing *dhuniyā grahe utapanno Dādū mahāmuni*[12]. This verse is often quoted in the controversies about Dādū's origin and can be translated in two ways, on account of the double meaning of *dhuniyā:*

'Dādū was born from the womb of a *dhuni* woman,'

or

'Dādū was found in a river.'

Two manuscripts used for the edition of Rajab's *Sarvāṅgi* (F and J, dated 1790 AD) give the reading *dariyā madhye utapanno mahāmuni*, in which *dariyā* can only be translated as 'river'.

Further, the *Bhaktamāl* of Rāghav Dās (1720 AD), with a commentary by Chatur Dās (1800 AD), is a gigantic work dealing with about twelve hundred *bhaktas* and devotees. The Nābhādās *Bhaktamāl* mentions only about six hundred Sants. Orr gives the following description of the work of Rāghav Dās:

(8) P.H. Śarmā:1936, vol. 1:3, p. 93, 129.
(9) Sv. N. Dās:1975, pp. 5-6.
(10) Orr:1947, p. 209.
(11) Nāhaṭā:1965, pp. 275-9.
(12) Callewaert:1978, p. 81.

"The Bhaktamal, completed in 1713, is one of a number of similar works modelled on the more famous Bhaktamal of Nabhaji, written about a century earlier. Ragho's poem, like the original, is often concise to the point of obscurity, and assumes on the part of the reader some previous knowledge of the events related. It is in fact, as its name suggests, an aid to memory, being primarily intended as a devotional manual. It has indeed another purpose - namely, to give Dādū his rightful place in the roll of saints. The main body of the work is non-sectarian, the bulk of its material being borrowed from Nabhaji; but interest naturally centres in Dādū and his followers, and the subsequent history of the Pantha ... (The Commentary of Chatur Dās) is now generally incorporated in modern versions of the Bhaktamal; but copies of the older work without commentary may still be seen"[13].

The work was edited by A. Nāhaṭā (Jodhpur, 1965), mainly on the basis of two manuscripts, dated 1804 and 1829 respectively. The text has both the original version of Rāghav Dās and the commentary by Chatur Dās[14]. Another edition was prepared by Swami Nārāyan Dās (Pushkar, 1969), with his own commentary "because the first edition appears to be full of mistakes." Nārāyan Dās used nine manuscripts, dated between 1783 and 1879.

In the report on my search for Dādūpanthī manuscripts, I have given 1720 AD as the date of compilation of the Rāghav Dās *Bhaktamāl*[15]. The date *samvat satrah sai satrahotarā* at the end of the work[16] was translated by Śarmā as Samvat 1770 (1713 AD) instead of Samvat 1777 (1720 AD)[17]. Both editors of the *Bhaktamāl* translate *satrahotarā* not as 77 but as 17, which would make the work much earlier, i.e. Samvat 1717 or 1660 AD. This early date (1660) looks improbable, and is also contradicted by the following discipleship lineage given by Nārāyan Dās: 1) Dādū, 2) Bare Sundar Dās, 3) Prahlād Dās, 4) Haridās, 5) Rāghav Dās. The details about Dādū's origin, caste, etc. are in agreement with the *enlarged version* of Jan Gopāl's *Janma līlā*[18].

In my book *The Sarvāṅgī of the Dādūpanthī Rajab*, I have listed a total of twenty-three works dealing with biographical data about Dādū[19]. They range from c. 1620 AD to 1912. As stated above, most of these works repeat what Jan Gopāl wrote, but they also add a few further details. Only one example will be given to illustrate this. In Jan Gopāl's work, it is only said that Dādū was born in Ahmedabad in 1544 AD. Nowadays, a big annual festival is held at Narainā on the birthday anniversary of Dādū, which is said to be the 'eighth day of the bright half of Phālgun', i.e. about the end of February. This accurate date *(phālgun sukala astami)* appears for the first time in Ātmabihārī's *Śrī Dādū charitra* (about 1830).

Non-Sectarian and Western Sources

Besides the sectarian works which have been discussed above there are several sources which were composed outside the Dādūpanth. They are among the earliest sources available, and the information they give

(13) Orr:1947, pp.213-214.
(14) Nāhaṭā:1965, pp. 1-278.
(15) Callewaert:1973, p. 157.
(16) Sv. N. Dās:1969, p. 898.
(17) P.H. Śarmā:1936, introduction, p. 2.
(18) Nārāyaṇ Dās, *Bhaktamāl*, p. 8.
(19) Callewaert:1978, pp. 22-29.

about matters such as Dādū's profession as a cotton-carder is all the more important since these sources seem to be free of all sectarian bias. What is probably the first reference to Dādū outside the Dādūpanthi literature is found in a verse of Eknāth and is quoted in the Marathi work *Sakal sant gāthā*. In his poem on the Nānakpanthis, Eknāth says: *Nānakā ghar Dādū pinjāri nām japan...*[20] This can be rendered as: "The *pinjāri* Dādū is like Nānak in the meditation on the Name..."

The second non-sectarian reference to Dādū is found in *abhang* 4299 of Tukārām's *Gāthā*[21]. The dates of Tukārām are generally taken as 1598-1650 AD. Since Dādū died in 1603, the year 1635 seems to be a reasonably approximate date for this piece of information. It begins with the statement "Pride of caste has never made any man holy, says Tukā. The untouchables have crossed the ocean of life by God-devotion, and the Puranas sing their praise." Then follows a list of those who were saved in spite of their low caste or different religious faith. The list includes Gorā the potter, Rohidās the cobbler, Kabir the *momin*, Latif the Muslim, Senā the barber, Kānhopātrā the daughter of a concubine, Dādū the cotton-carder, Chokhā Melā and Bankā the untouchable, Jāni the maidservant and Mairālā, the low-caste woman. The *abhang* is supposed to be authentic. In it, Dādū is specially mentioned by Tukārām as a *pinjāri*, one engaged in the profession of carding (the loosening or breaking up of) cotton.

Another early reference is found in a Persian work called the *Dabistān-i-mazāhib*, written in the mid-seventeenth century AD. If the work was written about 1665 AD, as maintained by Blochmann, it is a relatively close witness of events:

> "Another sect is that of the Dādū Panthians. Dādū was one of the cotton-carders in the village Narainā, in the district of Marwar. In the time of the Padshah Akbar (who inhabits heaven) Dādū devoted himself to the state of a Durvesh, and assembled many disciples about him. He prohibited his followers to worship idols, to eat the flesh of any animal or to hurt any living being; but he did not order them to abandon woman and wife or to withdraw from all business of the world; but he left it free to anyone to give up or to cultivate the connection and the intercourse with men"[22].

The quotation not only confirms the statement in Tukārām about Dādū being a cotton-carder, but also throws light on the sect which was already in existence and known to outsiders for its rules governing external behaviour.

The first known account about the Dādūpanth written by a Western author is in H.H. Wilson's *A Sketch of the Religious Sects of the Hindus*[23]. The note by the editor introducing Wilson's account in the Journal of the Asiatic Society of Bengal (1837) says that Wilson's

(20) T.H. Avate, ed., *Sakal sant gāthā*, Poona, 1924.

(21) Tukārām, *Gāthā*, 2 vols, Bombay, Government Central Press, 1950; 1:594.

(22) D. Shea and A. Troyer, eds, *Dabistān-i-mazāhib*, 3 vols. (Paris, 1843), vol. 2:233.

(23) The article (first published in *Asiatic Researches*, 16 (1828), pp.79ff.) was reprinted as a preface to the contribution made by G.R. Siddons, "Extract and Translation of one of the Granthas, or sacred Books, of the Dādūpanthi Sect,2 " in the *Journal of the Asiatic Society of Bengal* 6 (1837), pp. 481-87 and pp. 751-56.
These excerpts are the first known English translation of any Dādūpanthi literature. Wilson's article was later reprinted in H.H. Wilson, *Religious sects of the Hindus*, (1861), 1958, pp. 57-58.

"notice of the sect was chiefly obtained from Lieut. Col. Smith and partly from verbal information at Benares, where the elder branch of the same dissenters, the Kabirpanthias, have a principal establishment."

This account by Wilson is very important since the data given in it ("at Benares") will be found in most subsequent articles on Dādū in English for nearly a century afterwards, with only a few minor additional details.

In *The Sarvāñgi of the Dādūpanthi Rajab*, I refer to twenty-four such works or articles published after Wilson's article, which give descriptions of the origin of the Dādūpanth, the contemporary situation and the growth of the military branch of the Dādūpanth (the Nagas)[24]. Wilson calls the Dādūpanth "one of the direct ramifications of the Ramanandi stock; its founder is said to have been a pupil of one of the Kabirpanthi teachers, and to be the fifth in descent from Rāmānanda, viz. 1. Kabir; 2. Kamal; 3. Jamal; 4. Bimal; 5. Buddhan; 6. Dādū[25]."

Orr applied a critical test to some oral traditions about Dādū and gave a summary and analysis of Dādū's teaching, with a translation of many representative verses. His study of Dādū's life is divided into two parts.
- In the first part, 'The Life of Dādū in Tradition' (pp. 26-44), the narrative "is based almost entirely on a little work entitled 'The Life Story of Dādū'" (p. 26). Although Orr observes that "this poem has undergone considerable revision at the hand of later editors" (p. 26), he fails to distinguish the earlier accounts from those of later editions.
- In the second part (pp. 45-59) Orr critically examines the historicity of four points which have given rise to some debate:
  - Dādū's birthplace,
  - his caste and profession,
  - his religious teacher,
  - his interview with Akbar.

The abundance of additional information which Orr includes seems to be presented with a critical mind, but would have been much more valuable if the sources had been mentioned regularly. It seems as if he has gathered most of his information from oral informants who in turn relied mainly on sectarian sources and oral traditions.

Finally, a synopsis of biographical data relating to Dādū and commonly accepted in the *panth* now, is given in the *śri Dādū Mahāvidyālay rajat jayanti Grantha*, a memorial volume, on the 25th anniversary of the foundation of the school, in Jaipur (1919-1944), published in 1952. I summarize the description given in the *Introduction:*

> On the eighthday of *phālgun sudi samvat* 1600 (1543 AD), Dādū was found in a basket on the Sabarmati river, near Ahmedabad, by the *nāgar* brahmin Lodirām.
> At the age of eleven, near the Kānkariyā tank, an old *mahātmā* appeared to him and instructed him. A few days later, Dādū left his home and went to Peṭalād, where he met Mānak Dās and Gyān Dās; then he travelled over Ābū and Sirohi to Kalyānpur where he stayed for six years.. Then he travelled over Ajmer, Bhilvārā and Cittor to Karauli and then to Sāmbhar; he was about 19 years old then.

(24) For more details, see Callewaert 1978, pp.34-56.
(25) Wilson, *loc. cit.* See *Ibidem*, p. 32.

In 1562, the composition of the *Vāṇī* was begun and at the age of 25 Dādū started to preach.
He encountered opposition from the local Qāzīs and Hindu priests; people were forbidden to see him.
In 1569, Bare Sundar Dās of Bikaner became his disciple; many other disciples soon followed Dādū. He stayed in Sāmbhar from 1562 till 1574. His father's brother, Ānandī Rām Nāgar came to see him there.
In 1575 he went to Āmer, where Bhagavant Dās, the father of King Mān Singh was the ruler. Several disciples joined him there.
Mohan Dās Daftari started writing down his sayings. King Bhagavant Dās persuaded Dādū to accept Akbar's invitation to go to Fatehpur Sikri, about 1587 AD.
Afterwards, he travelled again around Rājasthān and in 1590 he left Āmer, for Āndhī (two years), Kalyān (one year) and other places in Rājasthān. In 1598 he went to Narainā where he sat down underneath the Khejarā tree.
He died there on the 8th of *jeṭh badī* and was exposed to the wild beasts, near Bharainā, on a place now called *Dādū khol*.

The two most recent works of biography on Dādū and the early history of the *panth*, have been produced by the prolific writer Svāmī Nārāyan Dās: *Śrī Dādū charitāmrit*, Ajmer, 1975, 2 vols, 580 and 558 pp. and *Śrī Dādū panth parichay*, Pushkar, 1979, 3 vols, 952, 1032 and 951 pp.

Manuscripts of the Dādū Janma Līlā

During my search for Dādūpanthī manuscripts in North India[26], I copied several manuscripts of the *Dādū janma līlā*, on the basis of which this critical edition was prepared[27].
In the colophons or in the description of the Mss., the following dates (here all expressed as AD) were noted:

A 1653 Narainā, 'private copy'; till verse 12.32; 12 fo.
C 1658 Vidyā Bhūśan Sangrah, Jaipur, 34; fo. 473-485.
D 1666, DMV, Jaipur, *guṭakā* 33; 20 fo. at the end of the Ms.).
G 1711, DMV, Jaipur 43.

B 1654 (Narainā 2, fo. 180-207).
E 1739 (Narainā, no number, 22 fo.).
F 1700 (?; Narainā 40; fo. 11-27).

The number of verses in manuscripts ACDG, in manuscripts BEF and in the Sukh edition vary considerably.

	ACDG	BEF	Sukh
ch. I	18	44	67
ch. II	18	21	26
ch. III	25	29	37
ch. IV	22	48	59
ch. V	28	36	37
ch. VI	28	28	40
ch. VII	28	42	53
ch. VIII	24	47	61
ch. IX	27	43	56

(26) See Callewaert:1973 and Callewaert:1977.
(27) For the works of Jan Gopāl, found in manuscripts now available, see Callewaert:1980, pp. 28-38.

ch. X	28	32	40
ch. XI	21	32	42
ch. XII	29	34	43
ch. XIII	31	44	56
ch. XIV	34	43	53
ch. XV	35	73	90
ch. XVI	29	30	36
Total	425	626	796

Note

Jan Gopāl has not produced a literary masterpiece. The rhyme, *e.g.*, is not perfect as appears from the samples below. Several times, the incorrect rhyme in Mss. ACDG is corrected in the version of Mss. BEF.

2:10 भाऊ । पांऊं
4:2 दषिन । बिचछन
4:5 सिरहांनैं । बषानै
4:6:6 हाथ । मात
5:6 तीनी । चींन्हीं
7:21 हाथी । संगाती
8:12:1 बमेको । बसेषी
9:17 आंबैरी । फेरी (14:8)
10:22 जाई । नांहीं
12:5 जांहिं । बांहीं
13:14:2 भई । दुही
14:33 तीनी । कींनीं
15:14 देषी । बमेकी
15:14:1 ठांई । जांहीं
15:18:6 हाथ । गात
15:23 गोरं । ठौर
15:34 राचै । बांचै
16:8 पूंन्यौ । दून्यूं
16:17 ज्ञानौ । ध्यांनु
16:27 सांही । जांही

Important intentional variants in the Dādū Janma Līlā

When we compare the text of Mss. ACDG with the text in Mss. BEF and in the Sukh Dayāl edition, we notice that the original text has been tampered with, especially with regard to the delicate questions of Dādū's non-Brahmanic origin and his occupation as a cotton-carder.
The earliest version (ACDG) clearly and merely states that Dādū was born in Ahmedabad and that he was working as a cotton-carder (*dhuniyā*). Thus in verse 1.6 of ACDG we read:

"There was great joy in the house of the *dhuniyā* (at his birth)."

In BEF and Sukh, however, we read instead:

"*All* were overjoyed."

Then follows an interpolation in both BEF and Sukh telling the story of the Brahman merchant in Ahmedabad who found a baby in a river. In Sukh, we are told that this merchant's name was Lodirām. This name is also found in the Rāghav Dās *Bhaktamāl*.
In v. 1.16 we read in Mss. ACDG: "He carded cotton", for which Mss. BEF give: "He entered the state of *sahaj*".

In chapter 2 the encounter with the Qāzi from Ajmer provokes a discussion which may imply Dādū's affiliation with the Muslims. In v. 11 we read: "A Muslim lives by the Divine Word". If this is a definition of the behaviour expected from Dādū, it is neatly avoided in Mss. BEF: "without the Divine Word, one cannot go to heaven".

Yet another example of variant readings is in the context of a burglary in Dādū's house. In verses 3.9-10 of ACDG we read:

> When the thief found threads (of cotton) ... the family awoke; (Dādū's) mother and wife said...

In BEF and Sukh we find instead:

> When the thief found books, the saints awoke;... the saints and disciples said, ...

Verse 4.5b in ACDG ("he went on carding cotton") is missing in both BEF and Sukh.

We find hardly any variant in the next chapters, till surprisingly the issue of cotton-carding is raised in the presence of Akbar. For "Working hard day and night, there are plenty of cotton-carders in Sikri" (in Mss. ACDG), we read in Mss. BEF :"Roaming around in a holy dress, there are many beggars in Sikri" (7.12).

The terms used in the interpolations of BEF to denote Dādū's birth clearly suggest that he was of divine origin: "He transformed His body and appeared in the form of a child", "He descended (*avatār lenā*)." For more references, we refer to the Concordance below.

In verse 1.7 of ACDG we read:

> 'When he was eleven years old, Bābā Būḍhā appeared to him'.

In Mss. BEF we read:

> 'Hari appeared to him in the form of an old man'.

The term *būḍhā* may be used in its literal, non-specific sense meaning 'an old man', it may be an actual name, or it may designate a particular person bearing the name as a title of respect. There is no certainty about the identity of this person, but there is definitely a difference between the reading *Bābā Būḍhā* (in the earliest version) and the literal meaning of *būḍhā* (as in the text of Mss. BEF). This difference is emphasised by the fact that Dādū's second-generation disciple Sundar Dās, when tracing the origin of the Dādūpanth back to Brahmā, calls

Dādū's preceptor Vriddhānanda.

Discussing the identity of Dādū's spiritual preceptor, Orr remarks:

> "the belief that Buddhan was a historical person is very general among members of the Pantha... We have incontrovertible evidence of the presence in Sambhar (where Dādū stayed at one time) in the time of Akbar, of a Muhammedan saint of this name, whose lineal descendants still have their home in Sambhar"[28].

Variants in verse 10.15 point to a very interesting turn in interpretation in the early *panth*. It looks as if there was very soon a tendency among Dādū's followers to adopt children at an early age. According to the reading in Mss. ACDG Dādū sees this custom as a condemnation of child-marriages leading to widowhood (see v. 10.18).

> One should not impose marriage on young persons who will get the blame (ACDG).

In the revised version (BEF) the argument is less sharp:
> The King listened quietly, with folded hands.

Additions and omissions in Mss. BEF

The additions refer to more miracles or give a special interpretation of a controversial issue. Often the interpolated verses do not fit in the flow of the narrative, or in the numbering of the verses.

- To the sober report in ACDG about Dādū's birth (1.5), Mss. BEF add 3 verses, hinting at the *avatār* aspect of Dādū's appearance:

> He appeared in a body,...for the sake of devotion *Hari* began this *līlā*,... the suffering world found new life,... holy persons appear at Hari's order, and fulfilling their task of devotion they enter again into Hari.

After 1.6 ("there was joy in the house of the cotton-carder"), we find 9 additional verses in BEF, with the account of the miraculous adoption by a merchant in Ahmedabad (his name is, however, not given); "He transformed His body into the form of a child,...He became an *avatār*..."
- 1.11: The initiation is symbolically described through a roll of *pān*, and Mss. BEF add: "He appeared everywhere and all creatures started to sing Dādū Dādū".
- 2.22: The encounter with Siddhas is related only in BEF.
- In chapter 4 we witness the painstaking efforts made in the enlarged version to 'explain' Dādū's association with the low-caste *dhuniyās*. In Mss. ACDG we read clearly and unambiguously:

> At first he lived as a cotton- carder, but later he accepted food as alms (4.3b).
> He never stopped carding cotton, when ordinary people or even kings came to see him; he went on carding cotton, sitting at the head of his bed, although the *dhuniyā* caste is considered mean (4.5ab).

In Mss. BEF, great pains are taken to compare Dādū to Kabīr and to suggest that he tried to associate with the lower castes in order to

(28) Orr:1947, p. 54.

avoid crowds. Apparently very soon in the early *pantha*, the relationship with the *dhuniyās* was considered not fitting to Dādū's status as a guru.
- In chapters 5-8 we find the dialogue between Dādū and Akbar and people at his court. The additions here are of a different kind, emphasizing Dādū's superiority, even over Akbar.

With folded hands Akbar bowed his head:
"Never have I heard such a reply.
I questioned him on the six systems
and nobody ever gave me such an answer". (5.27:2)

From that moment Akbar stopped hurting living beings,
since he had found Dādū, the excellent *pir*.
He made his decision into a religious law,
that no one should hurt living beings[29].
Akbar's attitude of mercy
did not suit the Qāzis and the Mullās.
They all agreed they should try
to reduce Dādū's power.
They prayed to the Prophet:
"Beloved, please take note of that power.
You have helped us with clear instructions;
please perform a miracle for us".
Akbar had a throne prepared
on which no other person was allowed to sit.
He was eager to see with whom real power was.
'Who knows the ways of the Unknowable?'
The throne was nicely arranged and
king Bīrbal[30] was sent to Svāmiji.
The King invited Dādū,
who already 'knew' what was happening.
"Why have you come", Svāmiji asked.
"I was sent to invite you", the King replied.
Svāmiji saw his inner thoughts
and disclosed what was being planned.
Abdul Fazl and King Bīrbal stared at
Svāmiji, in wonder.
He said: "You may go and say
that I am coming; do not worry".
Svāmiji then became the embodiment of love and took his disciple Jaggā with him.
Via a secret road he went to the emperor,
who was greatly astonished at what he saw.
A strange throne appeared in the sky,
radiating bright light and splendid beauty.
Svāmiji sat on it, like
the Highest-above-all, the Indweller.
Akbar was terrified:
Who can know the ways of Dādū?
The emperor came down from his throne, bowing low:
"You are the Master, I am your slave".
With this miraculous display,
the ignorance of the emperor disappeared:
"I am satisfied, God has appeared,
my doubts have gone". (7.25:1-11)

(29) This is clearly a later addition. The injuction not to harm living beings does not follow logically from Dādū's earlier statements in this context.

(30) See below, Ch. 2, verses 5.6ff.

King Birbal clearly showed his humility,
he took off his turban and put it at Svāmiji's feet:
"You make me feel very shy,
I can't possibly approach Gosvāmi."
Svāmiji felt pity for him and
placed the turban on his own head, upside down:
"I load the three worlds on my head
and the Creator will take away your shyness". (8.12:2-3)

When he saw his disciples hungry,
Svāmiji miraculously ordered a plate.
The food the disciples had asked for,
came floating on the water'. (8.17:2)

A *yogi* sat on a rock and made it float,
relying on the promise of the King of fishes.
Dādū's disciple Ṭīlā spoke out and
made the rock fly in the air.
Ṭīlā then felt pity and
made the rock and the *yogi* come down again.
The *yogi* fell at his feet,
and begged to be made Dādū's disciple. (8.19:2)

Seven hundred merchants sat in their ships,
carrying goods worth millions.
While crossing the ships got stuck in the river.
In the Ḍhūnḍhār region King Mān
had helped to promote the *bhakti* of Rām.
Rajab: the merchants called the Name,
and the ships could move again.
One day, in the Himalayas,
king Birbal was caught in an avalanche.
It happened in a valley of Kashmir,
where one should not make noise.
Not giving attention, the King had shouted,
and the snow came down with deafening noise.
Remembering his promise, Dādū
rescued him without delay.
Earlier, King Birbal had put his head on Dādū's feet,
and had asked for total protection.
'If anyone seeks Dādū's protection,
he will not fail to find the ultimate state'.
One day, Dādū's subtle body travelled,
witnessing an infinite variety of worlds.
A divine voice sounded, and resounded
as if having no end:
Beyond Beginning and End,
there is the Unparallelled Reality[31]
without form,
existing in itself, faultless:
no one knows its secret'.
'Indestructible, without beginning or end,
untouched by suffering.
See and serve Him in your heart, *Dādū*.
Only very few know His secret'. (8.23:1-7)

(31) *Anūpam dev*.

An interesting omission in Mss. BEF (verse 9.1b) makes an ambiguous context to be understood in a particular (sectarian) way. In the first lines of chapter 9[32] the account leaves us with the vague impression that Dādū's fatherhood is, like so many events in his life, the result of God's 'Unknown Ways'. The addition in Mss. BEF of 9.1:1-2 clearly points to a miraculous intervention: And that is the interpretation still current in the modern Dādūpantha. The next line (9.1b, missing in BEF) suggests that we cannot know how one 'gets' a child. Does the vague, first line of chapter 9 suggest that, at the time of composition of the *Līlā*, two theories were current in the developing *pantha*? One: Dādū had children in a human way, two: his children were conceived miraculously. I should add that it is not at all surprising that the early followers used the literary device of a 'special birth' to emphasize Dādū's greatness. Isn't that a popular device in all religions? Or should we, already at this stage, look for traces of asceticism in the early *pantha*?

In the last chapters of the *Līlā*, we find a few interesting interpolations (Mss. BEF), which emphasize the divine aspect of Dādū's personality:

> Dādūji said: "Brothers, keep my body
> and for whatever you ask, you shall get a reply.
> If you fear that my corpse will smell, remember
> that it is not composed of the five elements.
> If anybody still doubts,
> let him rub his hand on my body and see.
> My body is not real,
> like a reflection in a mirror."
> When they rubbed their hand over his body
> they felt it was like a flame from a lamp.
> They saw his body but could not grasp it with their hands
> and they were astonished. (15.18:4ff.)
> When there were no waters and no sun,
> even then Dādū Dās already existed. (15.18:21)

Names for God

Two names for God occur very frequently in Jan Gopāl's account: Hari and Rām, both used in a very *'nirguṇ'* meaning. The term *nirguṇ* itself is used rarely, and only in the later version of Mss. BEF:

> If you stay firm in the *nirguṇ* devotion,
> the Unknown will help you,
> and there will be no room for the corruption of a personal deity (*iṣṭa*) (15.18:13).

The relation to a 'personal deity' is somewhat clarified in two other verses:

> If a person is firm in his devotion to a personal deity,
> Rām will help him (15.18:18),

and

> The *nirguṇ* devotion will never be destroyed,
> as long as Brahmā, Vishnu and Śiva are worshipped (15.18:19).

For more references to *iṣṭa*, see the Concordance. See also v. 4.6:5 and the quotation of Rajab (15.31:2; only in Mss. BEF).

(32) This chapter 9 is itself possibly an interpolation or an oral account inserted by Jan Gopāl. See below, English Translation, chapter 9, note 1.

We also find the term 'Name', which is common in the poetry of the Sants and of Dādū.

> He meditated deeply on the Name (2.2). If a devotee has the Name of Rām in his heart, Hari will do exactly what that person asks Him (4.6:11). We meditate on the Name of Hari and controlling the senses we glorify Rām (5.12). He wanted to go far away and meditate in solitude on the Name (6.12). The King understood that all is empty without the Name of Rām (11.1:1). The Name of Rām is my sect. (12.3). He made his disciples firm in the devotion to the Name' (15.18:1).

After the introduction 'He has no name', we find in chapter 5 of the *Dādū Janma Līlā* the beautiful Litany of Names of God-without-Names:

> For our own satisfaction we give Him names,
> according to the qualities we discover in Him.
> Because He shows mercy, we call Him Dayāl (5.14...), etc.

Another favourite term[33] with Jan Gopāl is Brahmā.
We further also find Gosvāmi (1.1, 7.10f.), Govinda (1.6:5; 6.16), Antaryāmi (the Indweller), Param Puruś (1.8), Parameshvar, Kartār, Kartā, Sirjanhār, Raham, Bisambhar, Jaganāth, Murāri, Karanhār, Abigati, Ātma-Rām (see 1.13, note), Bhagvān (1.15, 11.15), Cintāmaṇi, Banvāri, Jagdis, Brahma, Pārbrahma, Pūran Brahma, Anabhai (see v.2.3, note), Nirañjan, Sāhib, Param Gur Rāi, Samartha, Khudāi, Param Guru (13.23), Guru (12.11),
See also the term Rām *ras* (the nectar of Rām; 1.1, 3.7, 4.4, 6.5).

The following terms are found only in the version of Mss. BEF: Nijānanda, Svāmi (9.1:2), Indestructible King (13.5:6), Gusāi (13.5:8), Adhar[34] (1.6:3, 15.18:2,) Dayāl (15.31.3), Abigati (15.18.13).

Several passages and phrases (especially in the BEF additions) are familiar to the reader of the Bible and the Gospel narratives.

> Early in the morning the merchant went to the river and a small child came floating by. He took the child home and his wife's breasts filled with milk (1.6:3)[35].

> They mocked: "What miraculous power do you have now? Saviour of the world, you are lost" (3.16).

> Eventually, Ṭīlā pointed out to Svāmiji that the sacred offerings were running out. The thoughtful teacher Dādū made the offerings again to arrive in plenty (9.12:3).

> If you fear that my corpse will smell, remember
> that it is not composed of the five elements.
> If anybody still doubts,
> let him rub his hand on my body and see.
> My body is not real,
> like a reflection in a mirror.
> When they rubbed their hand over his body,

(33) For the references to the lines giving these Names of God, see the Concordance. Only the terms Rām and Hari are not listed there.

(34) See Callewaert:1978, p. 238, v. 43.54.

(35) We should here refer to the double meaning of *dhuniyā: 'dhuni* woman' and 'river (see above, note 10).

they felt it was like a flame from a lamp.
They saw his body but could not grasp it with their hands
and they were astonished (15.18:4f).

This 'miracle' has to be understood in the context of Dādū's *avatār* (see above).

Interesting also is his encounter with animals: elephants (3.6; 7.21, 12.5), cows and oxen 15.6:1.

Dādū's disciples

More than one hundred disciples, devotees and ascetics are mentioned in *Janma Līlā*. We find only occasional additions (usually miraculous accounts) in the interpolated versions of manuscripts BEF.

Svāmi Nārāyaṇ Dās closely followed Jan Gopāl's account when he wrote his *Dādū Caritāmrit*, here abbreviated as DCA. Repeatedly I refer (between brackets) to the relevant pages in DCA, for those readers who are eager to know the oral traditions about each of the persons mentioned in the *Janma Līlā*.

1.6.5 Mohan Dās (?; only Mss. BEF; see footnotes)
1.6.6f. Jaimal (only Mss. BEF)

4.18 Santa Dās, Damodar, Garīb Dās, Dvārikā Dās
4.19 Cāndā, Ṭīlā, Jagjīvan, Śyām Dās (Lāhorī), Jagdīs Dās
4.20 Gun Dās (see note) and Dharma Dās
4.21 Mādhav Dās (see 4.6.11), Rāghav Dās

6.24 Cāndā

7.7 Jan Gopāl, Jagjīvan

8.17 "seven co-travellers"
8.17.1 Jaggā
8.18 Lākhā Narhar, Damodar (DCA 565)
8.19.1 Ṭīlā

9.2f. Garīb Dās (DCA 600)
9.6 Maskīn (DCA 600)
9.8 Santa Dās Gujarāti (DCA 605-607), Sāngā, Rām Dās, Dayāl Dās from Bairsal (DCA 609)
9.11 Narhar Dās, Mādhav Kāṇi (DCA 621, 627)
9.12.3 Ṭīlā
9.12.8 Mādhav
9.16 Damodar (DCA 643-644)
9.18 Pūrn Dās (DCA 668)
9.19 Jaimal of Sāmbhar (DCA 686)
9.20 Chājū; Hari Dās, Harisingh and Mohan (disciples of Jaimal; DCA 686-687)
9.21 Kapil of Chātsu (DCA 687-688)
9.23 Tolhā and Bāgar (DCA 688-689)
9.24 Lāl Dās of Āmer (DCA 690), Cetan, Keśav, Baghu (see 16.10), Dūjan
9.25 Mohan Dās of Pattan (DCA 690), Lāl Dās
9.26 Prāg Dās (DCA 690), Jhājhū, Bhagvān, Hari Dās and Gopāl, Mohan Dās of Mevār

11.1 Ṭilā (DCA 706)
11.10 Rāghav Dās, Pithā (DCA 726)
11.13 Tākū (DCA 733)
11.14 Mādhav Dās, Mohan of Reyān (DCA 738)
11.15 Narbad (DCA 746)
11.16 Kishansingh of Rāṭhor (DCA 764)
11.17 Sant Dās of Rewat (CDA 764)
11.18 Rāghav Dās of Rāni (DCA 766)
11.19 Mānsingh of Rāṭhor (DCA 769)
11.20 Rāghav Dās Cauhān; the brothers Prithvirāj and Lakhu (DCA 771/791)

12.5 Garib Dās, Rajab
12.8 Ṭilā (DCA 784-785)
12.9 Ḍurgā (DCA 785)
12.19 Lād Khān
12.20 Ishvar Kacchvāhā
12.22 Prāg Dās
12.23f. Sāh Tilok
12.28 Prāg Dās (DCA 800)

13.1 Gopāl Dās of Diḍvānā
13.3 Gopāl Jośi of Nāgaur, Rām Dās
13.6 Rajab
13.9 Bohith, Khem Dās, Ṭikā, Khetā, Tohā, Govinda
13.10 Ghaḍasi
13.12 Rāghav, Gobinda, Narāin (Rajab's disciples); Ṭhākur Dās
13.13 Govinda Dās
13.14 Ṭākū, Kanhai of Keśav
13.14.1 Ālhan
13.15 Jasvant, Jagannāth, Cāran Darsā
13.18 Kānhar Dās
13.19 Dūjan Sādh
13.20 Rūpā, Jitā, Lakhū, Bāi, Rāimal, Hāmā, Bāgh from Narbad
13.22 Rāy Singh
13.24 Baṛe Gopāl (DCA 871) Sindhū, Pipā, Candā, Bālā
13.25 Keśav, Bābā (or Bālā), Bhagvān, Mādhav, Santa Dās, Mohan Dās Daftari
13.26 Paramānanda, Kisna Dās (or Dūbariyā?), Moni, Dayāl Bengāli, Sādhū, Devendra, Vanmāli
13.27 Santa Damodar, Dayāl Dās, Paramānanda, Catur Dās Mardaniy, Jagannāth, Mohan, Ṭikā
13.28 Tejānanda, Mādhav, Vyās, Sukhānanda, Bāi Ramā (DCA 870) Catur, Jagannāth, Paramānanda
13.29 Catur, Bhagvān Dayālū, Rām Dās, Gopāl

14.1 Maheś Dās (DCA 884), Govinda, Lāl Dās, Damodar, Khem, Nādā, Sundar, Prem
14.2 Dāmodar, Ṭikā, Hari Dās
14.3 Bakhnā
14.4 Udhav, Mohan Dās
14.5 Taulhā
14.6 Laghu Gopāl, Ṭilā, Chitar
14.8 (Ben)
14.9.1 Mohan Dās Daftari
14.9.3 Ṭilā, Mohan Dās
14.10 Lāl Dās Māli, Dhārū, Rūpā, Paramānanda, Rām Dās
14.12 Rām Dās, Rānibāi, Biram
14.13 Haridās from Chātsū, Udhav Dās, Nārāyaṇ
14.14 Kārū, Kūmbhā, Narāin

14.15 Narāin (grandson of Dādū), Jan Gopāl, Cain (grandson of Dādū; DCA 1108)
14.16 Rām Dās, Mohan, Udhav, Deī Dās, Lakhnā, Sūdhav
14.17 Kānhādās (and his sister)
14.18 Nizām, Nāgar
14.19 Jan Gopāl, Janmunābāī, Sūrhari, Ṭīkā, Damodar, Bālāhari
14.20 Pīpā, Ṭhākur, Prayāg, Dayāl Dās, Caran Dās (of the Rānkā clan), Gansī
14.21 Rānā, Gāngā, Sāngā, Bhagvān, Rām Dās, Udhav, Keśav
14.22 Khem Dās, Mādhav, Chājū, Mathurābāī
14.23 Bohurā Narāin, Bhagvān Dās, Mādhav, Paṇḍā
14.24 Jagjīvan
14.25 Haridās (Yantrī, DCA 932), Bhagvān Dās
14.26 Lakhā, Narhari
14.27 Khivā, Narāin, Syāmdās, Harikhābāī, Hemī Banmālī, Tulsī
14.28 Dāmodar
14.29 Parbat, Bohith, Pūran, Garīb Dās, Khem Dās, Keśav, Devrāj
14.30 Caturā, Viṣṇu Dās, Dhyān, Balia (DCA 948)
14.31 Sūrahari, Caturbhuj, Rām Dās, Khem Dās
14.33 Mādhav, Rām Dās

15.1 Caturbhuj
15.2 Jaimal of Baurī, Kisna Dās, Prahlād (disciple of Śyām Dās), Pīpā
15.3 Kalyān Dās, Yādav, Tegvāru, Rām Dās, Dāmodar, Dūdā, Hari, Biram
15.4 Lakī Dās, Mādhav, Keśav, Dharam Dās
15.9.1f. Narāin Dās
15.10 Durjansāl
15.11 Amarā
15.14.3 Ṭīlā
15.16 Ṭīlā, Keśav, Govind Dās, Gopāl, Narhari
15.18.1f. Garīb Dās
15.21 Pīpā, Garīb Dās, Maskīn Dās, Gopāl, Narāin
15.22 Durgā, Dayāl Dās, Rajab
15.23 Ṭīlā
16.1 Garīb Dās
16.6 Sāngā, Jasā, Paharāj, Bohith, Dev, Khem, Dayāl Dās, Pīpā, Bisna
16.7f. Garīb Dās
16.10 Rām Dās, Baghā, Narāin, Devī Dās

Topography in the Dādū Janma Līlā

A summary of Dādū's life is given at the end of Jan Gopāl's account (16.26f.):

> Dādū spent twelve years as a child.
> Then he met his guru who appeared before him.
> In 1573 he came to Sāmbhar
> and in 1575 Garībdās was born.
>
> In 1585 he met Emperor Akbar
> and in 1593 he went to Kalyānpur.
> In 1602 he came to the town of Narainā
> and in 1603 he became one with Rām.

After his birth in Ahmedabad (1.5), we follow Dādū across Rājasthān, with the following biographical data and route. Interestingly, all data are given in the early version of Mss. ACDG. No topographical additions are given in the later version of Mss. BEF.

When he was 11 years old, Bābā Būḍhā appeared to him (1.7),
He did different works for seven years, and then Hari appeared to him (1.12),

From that moment he became indifferent to the world (1.14).
He left for *Sāmbhar* (2.1),[36]

Then Svāmiji decided to go to *Amer* (3.24),

Svāmiji started on the journey and was met by Jan Gopāl at *Sikari* (4.20),

The discussions (in Sikari) lasted for 40 days (7.1),

Svāmiji left the town (8.16),
Wherever he came, Sants of various sects sang his praise. With his seven co-travellers he stayed in the jungle, avoiding the villages for fear of the crowds (8.17),
In *Aulaudā* lived Lākhā Narhar and the devotee Damodar, who had given up all worldly concerns. From *Dyausā* Dādū was taken all around and great devotion was shown to him (8.18).
He finally arrived in *Āmer* (8.19).

In *Sāmbhar*, God had given him children (9.2).
Finally, Svāmiji arrived in *Āmer* and then, after one year the time came again to start travelling about (9.10),
In *Tonk* Narhar Dās organized a very popular festival (9.11),
He made his entry in *Guḍhalā* (9.13),
Svāmiji then returned to *Āmer* and made it clear he would not travel again (9.17),
He went to *Āndhi* (9.18), and then to Sāmbhar (9.19), (and back to Āmer, where he meets King Mānsingh, ch. 10).

The King asked how long Dādū had lived in Āmer. "For fourteen years now", Svāmiji replied (11.6).
The ascetic Svāmiji started on his wanderings, and
with firm mind his disciples accompanied him.
For about five days they were on the road;
with those fortunate disciples he halted in *Bhurbhurā* (11.9).
They stayed there for three months (11.10).
Svāmiji then came to *Kalyānpur*, he stayed for one year and left again, going westward for a couple of days. He arrived in *Pādū* (11.12-13).
Mādhav Dās invited him to *Khandāyā* (11.14),
Svāmiji came to *Tilānā* (11.16).

The King of *Bhuraṭiyā* near Bikaner heard that Svāmiji was in the area. He invited him to come immediately from *Khātū*, where Svāmiji had arrived. He had to call Svāmiji again from *Tosinā*, for nobody knew Svāmiji's plans (12.1-2).
Svāmiji proceeded to *Tosinā* and the monastery. This brought joy to the disciples. After two years had passed, he was invited to the Ḍhūḍhāhar region (12.18).
Then he went to *Ghāṭvā*, where Lād Khān served him for a couple of days. Celebrations of great devotion were held, and then Svāmiji went on his way again.
They went to *Kardauli* and on the way they visited *Sāhipur* (12.21-22).

(36) See below, v.9 .2

In *Rodhū* Svāmiji went to stay with the merchant Sāran (13.4), There he stayed for three months and then returned to *Mārwār* (13.5).
Rajab decided to organize a great festival and invited Svāmiji. He tried different ways to convince Svāmiji to come, saying that the Indweller would shower His grace on them. He urged him repeatedly, till Svāmiji gave the order for the journey and got on his way after a week. He blessed the saints he met on the way. The first stop was Alhanyāvās (13.7-9).
Via *Kārū* (13.10), they arrived in *Kevalpur* (13.11).
Ṭhākur Dās invited him to *Nilyā* (13.12), and then Svāmāji went to *Pādū* (13.14),
In *Pālari* was the house of the good devotee Kānhar Dās. Leaving all illusion, he surrendered (to Dādū) and found truth in his presence.

In *Īdawā* Dūjan Sādh lived near a pond, in the shelter of Hari (13.18-19).
He stayed in the monastery for a few days and then, at the Lord's order, he went his way. Being a fervent devotee, Rāy Singh learnt that Svāmiji was coming.
In *Tyaudh* he organized a great festival, full of devotion and of love for Hari.
The devotees of the Dhūndhar region begged Svāmiji to come (13.21-23).
After the first part of their journey, they arrived in *Sāmbhar* (13.31).

Bakhnā invited Dādū to *Narainā*... and Svāmiji stayed for a couple of days (14.3).
He was also invited to *Bharainā* by Udhav,... he further went to *Bacūn* (14.4).
Then Taulhā invited him to *Pūnyānā* (14.5).
Laghu Gopāl, Ṭilā and Chitar invited him to *Ratanpur* (14.6).
He was then invited by the queen of Rāṭhor and in *Āmer*, people were overjoyed (14.8).
Without prior notice Svāmiji arrived in *Karānjali* (14.11).
Biram invited everybody to *Sāngāner* (14.13).
They organized a fine festival of seven days, while camping at *Kānautā* (14.14).
Then Svāmāji went to *Kalyānpāṭan* (14.26).
In *Āndhi* lived the worthy Dāmodar (14.28).
Giving joy to all, Svāmiji left and went to see the devotees in *Thoharāi* (14.30).
Then via *Rāmhari* (14.31), he left for *Ratanpur* (14.32), and then took three days to go to *Sāmbhar* (14.33).
After that Dādū settled in *Kalyānpur* (14.34).

So now I'll speak of Dādū's fame spreading to the East and of the devotees who became associated with him (15.1).
He went to the celebrations in *Morḍā* (15.4) and returned to Kalyānpur and stayed there for one year (15.7).
He finally arrived in *Narainā* (15.11), where a monastery was built on the bank of the small lake, with a garden at the back, adjacent to the waters (15.14).

Quotations in the Dādū Janma Līlā.

Kabīr

According to Jan Gopāl's account Kabīr appears twice very prominently in Dādū's life, once at the beginning and once at the end:

Boundless knowledge of Divine Reality
dawned after he met the blessed Kabīr in *samādhi*,
and they discussed his doubts
about the divine experience.
He continually sang Kabīr's poems and verses
and became his equal in word and deed.
After his meeting with Kabīr,
he became an authority on Divine Reality (2.3-4).

When Dādū had settled at Narainā, at the height of his fame, he is said (only in the BEF account) to have an encounter with famous Sants (Nāmdev, Kabīr etc) and Siddhas. They have discussions all night (15.14:2).

For controversial issues in Dādū's life, the example set by Kabīr is quoted, e.g. when Dādū's association with the *dhuniyā's* is explained as an effort to find humiliation in the eyes of people, and also to organize peace for meditation:

He took to the profession of cotton-carding,
in the way Kabīr sought the company of a harlot (4.5:3; BEF).

In Mss. BEF we read about the miraculous way in which Dādū had children "As Kamāl was born to Kabīr" (9.1:1).

Kabīr too is said to be an *avatār*:

When there was no creation...
even then Kabīr, the servant of Rām was there... (15.18:22).

For references to Kabīr see also v. 15.31. Kabīr is several times mentioned in the context of other Sants, like Nāmdev, Raidās etc. (1.3, 4.6:1).

We also read "He seemed the incarnation of Kabīr" (1.17), and it is said that Emperor Akbar compares Dādū to Kabīr (4.8).

The following lines in the *Dādū Janma Līlā* are verses of Kabīr (the figures between brackets refer to the edition of P.N. Tivārī of the *Kabīr-Granthāvalī*, and the page refers to the translation by Ch. Vaudeville:1974).

7.20 (KG 11.8; p. 213)
10.12 (KG; p. 264)
10.15.2 (KG 30.5; p. 296)
10.27 (KG 19.11; p. 259)

Dādū

Most of the quotations from the *Dādū-Vāṇī* are found in the enlarged version of Mss. BEF (the figures between brackets refer to the Caturvedī edition):

2.7:1 (13.29); 2.7:2 (13.32); 2.11:1 (13.19); 3.22:3 (3.95); 3.23:1 (1.67); 4.20:1 (24.5); 4.20:3 (24.74); 5.26:3 (22.8); 5.27:1 (4.304);

6.3 (3.61); 9.11 (4.150); 10.13 (2.44); 10.21 (12.114); 12.13 (1.67); 14.33:4 (13.23); 15.8:1 (19.44); 15.18:11 (24.71); 15.18:12 (25.65); 15.18:15 (24.75); 15.18:20 (4.227); 15.24 (3.94 and 23.52); 15.31:4 (4.278); 15.31:5 (4.185); 16.23 (15.29).

Conclusions

On the basis of my research on the sources for the biography of Dādū and the history of the Dādūpanth, I have reached the following conclusions:

1. The earliest biography of Dādū (Jan Gopāl's *Dādū janma līlā*) has been changed and enlarged at a very early stage after its composition. Most interpolated details are encomiastic and miraculous. This fact emphasizes the need to work on reliable manuscripts.
2. Later biographies only add more details, which clearly grew out of the oral tradition. These additional elements seem to conform to an Indian archetype for the behaviour of Sants, which involves the performance of miracles in order to impress their audiences - even the Emperor Akbar.
3. In the early hagiography of Dādū, we notice a tendency towards Brahmanization. Although Dādū himself stressed that caste was not important, later disciples in the sect tried to hide his (possible) Muslim origin and Muslim preceptor and invented an explanation for his connection with the *dhuniyās* (cotton carders).
4. The basis for English writings (and recent Hindi writings) on the subject of Dādū and the Dādūpanth is Wilson's article of 1828. Relying mainly on informants in Benaras, Wilson started the tradition of calling Dādū a disciple in the lineage of Rāmānanda and Kabir.

CHAPTER 2

English Translation

chapter 1

1. I bow before the immaculate, divine Gosvāmī[1],
through my guru's favour I have been given all purity.
I greet all the Sants: through their devotion
I drink the nectar of Rām.

2. There is no end to the number of Sants
who appeared in the epochs *sat, tretā, dvāpar* and *kali*.
I sing of the celebrated one I have heard of
and bow my head to all the others.

3. Śiv, Sanak and his brothers[2],
Sukhdev[3], Dhruv and Prahlād[4],
Nāmdev, Kabīr, Raidās, Pīpā, Sen, Dhanā and Haridās,
they all served Hari.

4. May the other Sants take no offence
when I sing the praise of my guru Dādū.

 1. Wonderful is this story, difficult to express,
 how can a human tongue find the words?
 In the Vedas, Purānas and Qurān, this was never mentioned.
 Where can man find the words to describe it?

I have only one tongue and my mind is limited,
unable to express the innumerable events.

5. In the year 1544 AD a Santa was born on earth,
to the West of Ahmedabad, the holy man Dādū appeared.

(1) *Nirañjan*, *dev* and *gusāī* are here understood as epithets of God (see below, v. 7.11f.). *Gusāī* (Skt. *gosvāmī*) can also be understood as 'holy man'. See below, ch.7, v.11f.

(2) Lit.: 'Sanak and the others', which refers to Sanak, San, Sanatkumār and Sanandan, the four human sons of Brahmā. See Rāghav Dās *Bhaktamāl*, (Sv. Nārāyaṇ Dās:1969), p. 28.
In his *Dādū Caritāmrit* (pp. 138ff.) Nārāyan Dās:1975 relates how Brahmā (or Parameśvar or Hari) instructed his son Sanak to descend' *(avatār)* on earth, in the body of a person born in Ahmedabad, called Dādū, son of Lodhirām. The purpose of this descent is the revival of *nirguṇ bhakti* to Brahmā. The term *avatār*, referring to Dādū, occurs only in Mss. BEF (see below, Concordance).

(3) Śukadev, son of Vyās, is described in the *Bhāgavat Purān*, as an *avadhūt* or one who has discarded worldly obligations.

(4) For the information current in the early Dādūpantha, see Sv. Nārāyaṇ Dās:1969, pp. 47,70 and 93,145 respectively.

1. At the order of Nijānanda[5], the eternal, infinite
Brahmā, he appeared in a body.
Fulfilling the expectations of all living beings and
for the sake of devotion, Hari began this *līlā*.
2. Increasing the Lord's glory with his word, Dādū came.
The suffering world found new life, enjoying his presence.
3. As clouds appear in the sky,
accomplish their purpose and dissolve,
so holy persons appear at Hari's order,
fulfilling their task of devotion they enter again into Hari.

6. There was joy in the house of the cotton-carder[6]
as if the new moon had appeared.
His father and mother were very fortunate,
for their son was devoted to Hari.

1. There was a merchant living in Ahmedabad,
anxious to have a son.
One day he met an unknown holy man and
made him the following request:
2. "Hear my prayer, Svāmījī,
I am in great sorrow without a son".
Then a voice rose from the heart of the holy man:
"Go without delay to the river".
3. Early in the morning the merchant went to the river
and a child from heaven[7] came floating.
He took the child home and
his wife's breasts filled with milk.
4. Through the power of a *siddhi*,
He transformed His body into the shape of a child[8].
In this way Svāmījī left the royal throne and
in Mevār the seat of Mohan was seen[9].
5. He became an *avatār*
and the whole world was astonished[10].
His father and mother were overjoyed,
as if they had found Govinda that day.
6. Mukand Bhāratī had said:
"Mother, your Jaimal will not be my disciple[11].
An eternal, holy man has appeared;
he is Dādū, the guru of Jaimal.
7. Such a person has come
who will be able to liberate millions of people"[12].
Jaimal's mother said: "How can I find him?
Tell me how he is to be found".

(5) 'He who rejoices within himself'.

(6) We read in Mss. BEF: 'all Sants experienced joy'.

(7) *Bālak adhar*. *Adhar* can be understood as 'heaven' or as an epithet for God.

(8) It may be noted that even in Mss BEF no mention is made of Lodhirām, who is referred to in the Sukh Dayāl edition, ch.1.18.

(9) The term *mohan* is nowhere else in the *Līlā* used to denote God. If *mohan* refers to the disciple Mohan Dās (see 1.6.5, note), mentioned in the Sukh version, we could render the line as 'in Mevār Mohan saw his seat'.

(10) In the Sukh Dayāl edition (1.20b-32a) we read in this context how Mohan Dās became Dādū's disciple. After a shipwreck, Mohan Dās met a Santa who introduced him to Dādū in Āmer. With his *santa śakti* Mohan Dās arrived in Āmer, in the Rām Bāgh, and was made a disciple.

(11) See below, v. 4.6:2ff.

(12) Lit.: 'three crores'. For a similar idea, see the other 'interpolated' verses 4.6:3ff.

8. (Mukand replied): "Mother, hear my true words.
He became an *avatār* in Ahmedabad.
When he comes to Sambhar and Āmer,
go and see him".
9. The mother of Jaimal
kept the *gosvāmī's* words in her heart.
Day and night she was meditating on the question
when Svāmījī would come to Āmer.

7. When he was 11 years old, one day at dusk
while playing with other children,
Bābā Būḍhā appeared to him[13].

8. 'The Supreme Lord is sporting,
He grants liberation, the Indweller.
He crosses and guides one over the ocean of rebirth.
Wealth, perfection and liberation are always found in his court'.

9. The old man came and begged for money,
testing the discernment of every child.
Svāmījī gave without delay and the old man,
giver of all happiness, was pleased.

10. If a child shows such intelligence,
what love will he be capable of later?
The old man was happy,
he called the boy close to him and touched him.

11. He put a sweet *pān* roll in his mouth,
giving him everlasting knowledge of Rām.

1. One drop of *pān* fell on his feet and
at its touch, brothers, he was granted liberation.
He appeared everywhere and
all creatures started to sing 'Dādū, Dādū'.

He gave him everything, putting his hand on the child's forehead.
The child did not grasp what was happening.

12. Dādū did different works for seven years
and then Hari appeared to him.
He started to travel on the true path and
his mind turned from external things to the internal.

1. While his father was engaged in business on the sea,
Svāmījī started to preach Hari.
Whenever he met a Santa he gave away everything:
money, clothes and food.

2. He was turned out of the house, but
he did not take the family-share.
Preparing sweets he ate and gave them to eat
and he kept singing the name of Hari[14].

3. Svāmījī then made up his mind
to abandon the business of the world.

(13) In Mss. BEF we read: 'Hari appeared to him in the form of an old man'.
(14) The meaning of line 12.2b is not certain. See below v.1.16.

Leaving his family, home and homeland
he decided to sing the praise of his Creator[15].

13. He saw the splendour of the Divine Light,
while Rām-within[16] dwelt in his heart.
Later, a voice spoke from heaven:
"May the whole world know the blessed Dādū".

14. From that moment he became indifferent to the world,
day and night he meditated and reflected.
He made no distinction between ants and elephants[17],
gold and iron were equal to him.

15. Unmoved by praise or scorn
he saw the Blessed in all beings.
Detached from wealth and sexuality
he spent all his time in merciful acts.

1. The whole world gathered to see him,
but he was interested only in meditation.
Scorning the caste-divisions like dust[18],
he was immersed in Hari, like a son of God.

16. He carded cotton[19], ate and gave to eat.
In truth nothing disturbed his mind.
He gave without asking anything and
he liked to serve his own servants.

17. Mercy dwelt in his body,
he seemed the incarnation of Kabīr[20].
His lifestyle, speech and acts were truthful,
he was free of partiality and full of earnest holiness.

18. If one sings or hears the birth-account
of Dādū Dīndayāl,
undivided devotion to Jagdīs will come to him,
says Jan Gopāl.

chapter 2

1. He left for Sāmbhar, full of love,
but suffering *virah*.
He was yearning for the Supreme Brahma[21]
and the hidden light within him shone brighter.

(15) After these verses (interpolated in Mss. BEF), an additional episode is narrated in Ms. B (only), verses 32-37: Surrounded by dacoits Dādū appears in the form of an army; the dacoits seek his protection and are converted (see the Sukh Dayāl edition, 1.55-58).

(16) For *ātam-rām*, see Vaudeville:1969, pp. 62ff. For the use of *ātam-rām* by Rajab, see Callewaert:1978, p. 294.

(17) A similar expression -suggesting the totality of living beings- is found in the *Rajab-Vāṇi, ang* 78.20: "Do not heed evil thoughts against worms or elephants". Callewaert:1978, p. 257.

(18) Lit.: 'He called the *varṇāśram* a relation of mud'.

(19) In Mss. BEF we read the interesting variant: 'He entered the state of *sahaj*'.

(20) Lit.: 'as if Kabīr had come down' *(autare)*.

(21) *Pār-brahma*.

2. He meditated deeply on the Name,
with detached soul and composed body.
Beholding the light, glimmering or bright,
he realised his life was very successful.

3. Boundless knowledge of Divine Reality[22]
dawned after he met the blessed Kabir in *samādhi*,
and they discussed his doubts
about the divine experience.

4. He continually sang Kabir's poems and verses
and became his equal in word and deed.
After his meeting with Kabir,
he became an authority on Divine Reality.

5. He ignored all Muslim customs[23]
and abandoned Hindu practices.
He did not mix with other ascetics[24],
but stayed immersed in Rām day and night.

6. He abstained from hypocrisy, vanity[25],
partiality and sectarianism, knowing only the Supreme Brahma[26] as the total truth.
He rejected all temple-worship of gods, pilgrimages and fasts
and did not visit holy persons or shrines[27].

7. Both Hindus and Muslims began to clash with him,
but he had a ready answer for all.
Finally, Qāzis and Brahmans all gave up:
Hari was his protector, so what could they do?

> 1. 'If I do not adhere to Muslim customs,
> what does it matter to you?
> Who has said that such worship is essential?'[28]
> 2. 'When a boat is wrecked on the ocean
> and all are sinking,
> everybody flees to save his life, *Dādū*'.[29]

8. The Brahmans and Baniyas deliberated
and reported to the Council.
They wrote a letter and announced publicly
that people should take note of their decision:

9. "Anybody going to see Dādū
will be fined 500 Rupees".
The clerk wrote out the order correctly,
but the words were changed when the order was read:

(22) *Anabhai* has in contemporary literature the meaning 'mystical experience' and can here be understood as 'Divine Reality', which is the object of an experience.
(23) Lit.: 'he dug and buried the Muslim path'.
(24) Lit.: 'the six systems of philosophy'.
(25) The term *bheṣ* seems to denote the attire of a *saṃnyāsi* or the follower of a distinct sect.
(26) *Pūran brahma*.
(27) *Jāti* is here understood as a synonym of *jāt*. *Jāt denā* means: 'to visit a shrine with presents out of gratitude, or for asking a favour'.
(28) *Dādū-vāṇi*, Caturvedi ed., v. 13.29.
(29) *Dādū-vāṇi*, Caturvedi ed., v. 13.32.

10. "Anybody not going to see Dādū
will be fined 500 Rupees".
From that moment faith started to grow in Sāmbhar
and famous holy men came to see him.

11. A Qāzi came from Ajmer with the Qurān in his hands:
"Why have you upturned the true path[30]?
A Muslim lives by the Divine Word[31]
if a person calls on Rām he is an infidel".

1. 'An infidel is he who speaks untruth,
who does not keep his heart pure,
who does not recognize the Lord
and who is full of deceit, *Dādū*'.[32]

12. Svāmiji said: "Listen, Qāzi, why
have you been deluded by this deception[33]?
For the Muslim the basis is Religion *(dīn)*, while
the Hindu is equally zealous about his own conviction.

13. Which belief is agreeable to the Almighty,
if you know tell me quickly[34].
What Religion *(pantha)* can it be,
where creatures are killed?"

14. The Qāzi became furious and hit Dādū
blessed Svāmiji did not even try to protect himself.
When he received a blow on his other cheek,
Dādū said: "Now will happen as I tell you, brother.

15. The first blow was percieved in this world,
at the second blow the Creator came to know.
My body is very hard, Qāzi,
and your hand will go on aching".

16. The Qāzi, feeling ashamed, went home,
and the Almighty made his arm very painful.
The Qāzi thought: "I have sinned
hitting the Master[35] in the face."

17. Three months later the Qāzi died in great suffering,
but full of repentance.
He who harms a saint,
meets utter destruction.

18. A person will find liberation, if he sings or hears
this joy-giving story of the life of Dādū Dīndayāl,
says Jan Gopāl.

(30) Would this suggest that Dādū had belonged to the Muslim fold?

(31) Does this line suggest that for the Qāzi Dādū is a Muslim, who turns to Hindu gods? In Mss. BEF we read: 'without the Divine Word, one cannot go to heaven'. The variant clearly avoids the issue. See below, ch. 3.3.

(32) *Dādū-vāṇi*, Caturvedi ed., v. 13.19.

(33) This line suggests that Dādū is convinced that the difference between the Hindu and Muslim creeds is entirely on the illusory level.

(34) Line 13a is not found in Mss. AG. The numbering in these manuscripts is adjusted in v. 2.17a (not numbered), giving a total of 17 distichs in chapter 2, instead of 18 distichs as in Mss. CD.

(35) *Sāhib* is an epithet of God.

chapter 3

1. In Sāmbhar a proud Qāzī
intent on harming Svāmījī thought:
"I shall go to my village
and punish him.

2. I will dig a pit, bury him up to his neck
and pierce his head with arrows.
A musket, an arrow or a spear would be suitable,
a stony club or a hatchet should be fetched[36].

3. It is written in the Book:
'How can Muslims spread heresy[37]?
The truth of Religion *(dīn)* will remain firm,
if frauds and rogues disappear'".

4. That came to the attention of the Indweller,
for enmity with a saint is sure to end in adversity.
The Qāzī had 700 bundles of cotton[38] in his house:
it all started to burn, although there was no fire around.

5. The whole house burnt down
and the Qāzī was very frightened.
He no longer thought of harming Svāmījī,
but left him in peace.

6. Then Svāmījī came out of town,
totally concentrated on the Indweller.
A mad elephant came running towards him
and everyone with him fled.

7. Svāmījī had no fear at all,
since the Indweller was aware of his situation:
"This elephant comes, mad and intoxicated with illusion.
I continue to taste the nectar of Rām."

8. The elephant stood still and
seeing this the people experienced great joy.
The elephant bent down and touched the feet of Svāmījī,
who placed his hand on its forehead.

9. Another time, a thief broke into Svāmījī's house,
but there was nothing of value.
He found only threads[39] and starting to take them away,
made a noise which woke the family.

10. Dādū's wife and mother-in-law said[40]:
"What's happening? There is a man in the house,
he must be a thief because he doesn't reply".

(36) The meaning of this line is obscure. Nearly all words occur only once in this text.

(37) See above, ch.2.11, note.

(38) Seven hundred *man* or roughly 28,000 Kg!

(39) In Mss. BEF we read: 'when he started to take away books and pages...the disciples awoke'.

(40) In Mss. BEF we read: 'all the disciples said.... .

11. Svāmiji said: "Go away quickly, my friend,
while no one is fully awake.
If a watchman wakes up,
your death would grieve me".

1. The thief repented and said:
"This great soul has saved my life".
He took *prasād*, vowed to leave all stealing and
became his disciple.

12. When they saw Svāmiji singing hymns inside a temple,
the Qāzi and the Muslims were offended[41].
A crowd gathering all around
came and carried him away to kill him.

13. He kept the divine awareness constantly alive in his body,
but his outer skin became dead.
Usually[42] moving to give the rhythm,
his hands now were motionless by his sides.

14. Even in the presence of the evil, angry and sensual people,
Svāmiji kept beholding the Indweller.
Whether people honour him or beat him,
a holy man sees Rām in all.

15. He was taken to the commander-in-chief,
who would later suffer and repent his sin.
The commander was again[43] stubborn
and threw Svāmiji into a dungeon.

16. They mocked: "What miraculous power do you have now?
Saviour of the world, you are lost".
But the Almighty took pity on him,
like a mother on her suffering child.

17. Svāmiji appeared to all inside and outside the prison and
the darkness in which the commander was caught disappeared:
"Forgive me my sin,
how could I know your true nature?"

18. Svāmiji said: "You are not to blame,
whatever the Creator orders pleases me."
When the people in town heard this,
they arranged seven celebrations.

19. Svāmiji stayed at home, resting,
as if he did not know about the devotional celebrations.
The Creator performed a miracle, but
nobody understood the significance.

20. Whenever devotees came to take him somewhere,
Svāmiji's form appeared there.
Everyone derived much joy from the celebrations,
their affection increased and they enjoyed this display of love.

(41) See above, note to v. 2.11.
(42) The meaning of *man bhāvai te* is not certain.
(43) *Phuni* may refer to a previous action of the same officer.

21. Everyone tells this story
of Dādū's appearance in seven different places.
Svāmiji asked that the matter be given little attention:
only the Unknown knows His own ways.

22. Dādū's honour and renown increased everywhere
and people crowded to see him.

1. Two Siddhas came to him,
proud of their power to see (faraway) horses.
Svāmiji said: "What are you giving your attention to?",
and showed them (a horse with) blue ears.
2. "You haven't achieved anything supernatural[44] yet.
What is there in mastering a mere *siddhi?*"
The two Siddhas reported that the perfect guru
had put the mystic truth within their reach.
3. "There is no marvel in what you see,
but in what you cannot see.
Do not weep for what is visible
but for what is invisible, *Dādū*'.[45]

All the devotees[46] came to see him;
he mysteriously appeared to all of them in turn.

23. Then the question of dress arose
and Svāmiji was not pleased.

1. 'Like a garland strung on a thread,
the Sadguru has given me a mind controlled by breathing.
Not moving my hands I can pray day and night,
this is the highest recitation'.[47]

"How can I please the Muslims and
what should I wear for the Hindus?"

24. Then Svāmiji decided to go to Āmer,
which is a good place for meditation.
Jan Gopāl sings the well-known story of Dādū Dīndayāl:
whoever hears it knows the right way.

chapter 4

1. When Svāmiji came to Āmer[48],
the King and the people were overjoyed.
Day and night the crowds flocked to his house,
to hear devotional songs and narratives.

(44) For the rich meaning of *vastu*, see S.G. Tulpule, 'The *Vastu*, or the Reality of Medieval Indian Saints', in M. Thiel-Horstmann:1983b, pp.403-411.
(45) *Dādūvāṇī*, Caturvedi ed., v. 3.95.
(46) In Mss. CG we read: '*Rām*, *Gaṭā* (*Ghaṭṭ* in the Sukh Dayāl ed.) and Jangi came'.
(47) *Dādūvāṇī*, Caturvedi ed., v. 1.67.
(48) The ancient Dādūdvārā at Āmer is situated at the foot of the hill on which stands the Amber Palace. The Jaipur dynasty (under Sawāi Jai Singh II) moved to present-day Jaipur in 1733 (foundation in 1728).

2. From North, South, East and West,
the holy men and saints came.
All sorts of people came to see him
and offered gifts in deep devotion.

3. Svāmiji did not work,
for clothing and food were obtained easily.

> 1. Day and night big crowds were gathering and
> his meditation started to be disturbed.
> He then took up the occupation of a cotton-carder
> in an attempt to get rid of the crowds.
> 2. "If anybody wants to see me,
> let him look at my occupation."
> But the more Svāmiji tried to hide,
> the more people came to see him.
> 3. He adopted the humility of a servant,
> but a lamp cannot be hidden by throwing a shade over it.
> As Svāmiji tried to hide his glory,
> the Master increased it more and more.
> 4. 'As one pulls the string of merit lower,
> the lamp of knowledge rises sky-ward.
> Only the wise can understand
> this paradox[49], says Rajab'.

At first he lived as a cotton-carder,
but later he accepted food as alms.

4. He distributed cloves, dates, nuts and sweets
and did not store away any provisions.
Leaves and flowers were given away as they were received
and Svāmiji remained immersed in the nectar of Rām.

5. He never stopped carding cotton,
when ordinary people or even Kings came to see him.

> 1. People kept coming, begging to see him, knowing
> that he was fully occupied in cotton-carding.
> A voice came from heaven:
> "Stop carding cotton, the world will be destroyed.
> 2. People do not know your secret
> and they will go to hell despising you.
> That will be the result of despising you
> and in hell nobody can be saved."
> 3. From that moment Svāmiji stopped carding cotton,
> with undisturbed devotion he meditated on Brahma.
> He took to the profession of cotton-carding
> in the way Kabir sought the company of a harlot.
> 4. The more he tried to hide himself,
> the more Hari made him known.

He went on carding cotton, sitting at the head of his bed,
although the *dhuniyā* caste is considered mean.

6. 'If you do not give up this profession,
you'll lose Hari and evil will spread all over the world.'

(49) The image is probably drawn from the technique of kite flying: the more you pull, the more the kite rises.
For more information about Rajab, see Callewaert:1978.

1. Svāmi Dādū appeared like Kabir,.
Nāmdev, Dhruv and Prahlād.
When he came to Āmer,
the word about Jaimal was recalled to memory.
2. The *gosvāmi*[50] reminded the mother of the words about Dādū
and said that Svāmiji, the joy-giver, had arrived.
As soon as the *gosvāmi* had told her,
Jaimal's mother went to see Dādū.
3. She spoke to Svāmiji
as Mukanda Bhārati had told her to do:
"A saint will appear
who will cause the liberation of innumerable beings".
4. She said: "Blessed is the *gosvāmi* who gave me your name.
I have now come to see you.
He told me about your power and
praised your capacity to save millions of people."
5. Dādū said: "As long as heaven and earth exist, mother,
souls will be saved.
Via the bridge of *nirguṇ bhakti*,
the works of countless beings will be made perfect".
6. Svāmiji put his hand on Jaimal's forehead
and made him his disciple.
With mercy he touched his forehead and
Jaimal and his mother became detached from the body[51].
7. Leaving all worldly behaviour,
they became immersed in meditation on Hari.

A cheat falsely called himself Dādū,
but Svāmiji brought him to the service of Hari.

8. A rogue profited using the name of the great person,
but abandoned cheating and came to Dādū for refuge.
Mādhav Dās, the disciple of Svāmiji
settled in Sikari[52].
9. He sat quietly in front of a temple,
turning his back to the deity inside.
When people saw this they picked him up, saying:
"Who do you think you are - Nāmdev?"
10. What did Nāmdev do?
He produced milk and revived a cow.
Mādhav Dās was just as capable and
everyone saw that milk was consumed by the wall.
11. If a devotee has the name of Rām in his heart,
Hari will do exactly what that person asks Him.
Now, Tursi, the father-in-law of Mādhav Dās
was an evil-minded Brahman.
12. He was wretched with jealousy and
went to the Emperor to relate this story.
To stop Mādhav Bhāi,
the Emperor put him in á lion's cage.
13. Mādhav then concentrated on God,
the lion was frightened and kept away from him.
In the morning the Emperor enquired and
was told the lion was as scared as a cat.

(50) I.e. Mukanda Bhārati, see above, v. 1.6.1f.
(51) *Bideh*, lit.: 'without body'.
(52) See Rāghav Dās *Bhaktamāl*, p. 736.

14. That morning Akbar saw that
the saint was a man of Allah and
remarked: "This saint is remarkable".
Tursi's blood drained from his cheeks.
15. Akbar told Tursi to let Mādhav go and
to invite Mādhav's guru Dādū immediately.

7. When the Emperor heard about Dādū,
he sent him an invitation several times.
"If Svāmiji does not come,
the Emperor finds no rest."

8. Akbar told King Bhagvant Dās[53]:
"Your Svāmi is the giver of joy.
I have heard about his glory from many sources,
as if Kabir has come to live among us."

9. The King replied: "This saint does not go anywhere",
and Akbar asked: "Will he allow me to meet him, or not?"
The King then stood up and
requested the Emperor to be patient.

10. Back home the King regretted (his offer) and
confessed to the Almighty that he had been stupid.
He knew that under no circumstances Svāmiji would
come and the Emperor would be outraged.

11. With this doubt the King abstained from food
and drink, till Sūjā Khici heard about it.
"Give me the order and I'll go and get him,
this way I'll be able to see him myself."

12. The King gave him a letter straight away,
wrapped securely and closed with a seal:
"This is an urgent invitaton,
at the request of the Emperor".

13. Sūjā arrived in Āmer and
meeting Dādū he gained merit[54].
He gave him the letter and explained the message:
"Svāmiji, I have come to invite you to return with me."

14. Dādū replied: "Why should I come and what for, my friend,
I have no business with Kings".
Sūjā said: "Both the Emperor and the King insist,
saying that they will gain very much by seeing you."

15. "If you agree to go (to Sikari) I'll return home,
if not, I won't eat or drink."
Svāmiji: "You may return home, my friend,
what the Creator orders, will happen."

16. Svāmiji entrusted the matter to Rām and

(53) King Bhagvān or Bhagvant Dās was the heir of Rājā Bihar Mall and adoptive father of Mān Singh (see below, 10.1). He served in Akbar's army and died in Nov. 1589. The meeting between Akbar and Dādū was in 1585 (see below, 16.27). Bhagvān Dās is reported to have been the only person who expressed his misgivings about Akbar's plan to formulate and impose his 'Universal Religion'. See V. Smith:1966, p. 152-53.

(54) Lit.: 'he improved his birth'.

in meditation he was given the order to go.
He informed his disciples of his decision,
relying on Hari, his Protector in thought and speech.

17. "If I don't go he[55] will force me and
I shall be the laughing-stock of everyone "
Making preparations for the journey
he left instructions with his disciples.

18. Sant Dās was put in charge of the residence,
Damodar was to pass on his orders.
In the service of Garīb Dās,
Dvārikā Dās had to carry out the orders.

19. He took Cāndā and Ṭīlā with him
and entrusted the teaching to Jag Jīvan.
Syām Dās, who was also called 'Lāhorī'
and the disciple Jagdīs Dās accompanied him.

20. The disciples Guṇ Dās and Dharma Dās also came along[56].
Taking seven disciples with him,
Svāmījī started on the journey and
was met by Jan Gopāl at Sīkarī.

> 1. Together with all the saints he reflected
> on the importance of the request to meet the Emperor.
> Taking Nāmdev, Kabīr and Prahlād as his witness,
> he confirmed his decision.
> 2. 'When her husband is dead,
> the faithful wife burns with him;
> when he is alive she brings her house to him.
> A real *satī* is with Rām in life and death'.[57]
> 3. 'If we think life belongs to us,
> we are frightened when it disappears.
> Life belongs to Him and He will take care of it,
> *Dādū*'.[58]

21. Mādhav Dās was there already
and now came forward to see Svāmījī.
There were also the brother Rāghav Dās and Jaggā,
who had been the simple servants of the joy-giver.

22. Thus the departure of Dādū Dīndayāl to Sīkarī
is described.
Hari will be with him, who tells the story of the saints,
says Jan Gopāl.

(55) It is not clear whether 'he' refers to the Emperor or to God.

(56) The readings and meaning of this line are obscure. Ms. D gives *bānarā* instead of *bādarā*), while in Mss. BEF we read *sangi gunadās barā rajabaisi*. In his *Dādū charitāmrit* (p. 275), Svāmī Nārāyan Dās seems to follow the latter reading when he writes about Guṇ Dās *rāj-vamśi*, i.e. 'of royal descent'.

(57) *Dādūvāṇī*, Caturvedī ed., v. 24.5.

(58) *Dādūvāṇī*, Caturvedī ed., v. 24.74.

chapter 5

1. When Dādūji arrived in Sikari,
King Bhagvant Dās was informed.
Dādūji was brought into his presence and
for a couple of days was shown hospitality.

2. The King sent news to the Emperor that
Svāmiji, the joygiver had arrived.
The Emperor wanted to see him immediately, he was
even ready to come and see Dādū at the King's residence.

3. "With your permission", the King said,
"I shall bring him to your palace".
He then told Svāmiji
what the Emperor had said.

4. Svāmiji remarked: "Whatever Hari orders
-joy, grief or doubts- that very thing will happen".
He was taken to a hall with a log-fire and
the Emperor was informed about his arrival.

5. The King suggested he should prepare a few nice remarks,
to make a good impression on the Emperor.
Dādū replied: "The instrument is not important here,
since Rām is the musician".

> 1. 'If I forsake Rām, who will follow him?
> If I do not speak up, who will, says Dādū?'

6. The Emperor sent three advisors to question Dādū
about what is right and wrong, and
Abdul Fazl and Birbal[59]
came to talk to him.

7. The third person was the Brahman Tulsi,
who had given up the service of Rām to run after *māyā*.
"Hail to the King", he said when he entered,
but Svāmiji ignored his greeting.

8. "Hail to Him whom all the saints adore,
Whom moon and sun and earth and winds worship,
Whom gods and men praise,
Whom all celestial beings glorify.

(59) 'Nripati' or King Birbal is a very interesting figure. He was born as a poor Brahman and was at first in the service of Rājā Bhagvant Dās (see above, 4.8). "He was a member of Akbar's innermost circle of friends, rivalling in intimacy Abdul Fazl, whom the Jesuits called the emperor's Jonathan. Indeed, it is said that Birbal possessed the uncanny power of divining his master's secrets, a dangerous gift to which Abdul Fazl did not pretend. Akbar loved to have Birbal by his side, that he might enjoy his witty conversation" (V. Smith:1966, p. 170).
The presence of Birbal as negotiator between the Emperor and Dādū is all the more important because Birbal "was hostile to the Sikhs, whom he considered to be heretics" (*Ibidem, p. 171*). Considering Dādū's clashes with both Brahmans and Qāzis, one wonders how he figured in the encounter with Dādū. We only have Jan Gopāl's chronicle.
Smith further quotes Badaoni: "Bir Bar also, who had fled from fear of his life (in 1586, battle near Attock), was slain, and entered the row of the dogs in hell, and thus got something for his abominable deeds he had done during his lifetime" (*Ibidem*, p. 168).

9. Hail to the Unstained Rām-within[60].
To this one Father goes all my love.
How can I glorify what is false,
what is born and dies, and comes and goes?

10. A faithful wife only thinks of her husband,
A prostitute goes and gossips everywhere."
Tulsi was very ashamed and remained silent,
how could he show his face to Rām?

11. Then the Sheikh spoke: "Listen, gosvāmi,
you are like our elder brother.
Let us share in your wisdom, tell us
what god you worship and how you meditate?"

> 1. 'The Creator of heaven, earth and the lower regions,
> of all that has a beginning and an end,
> Who gives to all created beings,
> He is the god of our choice, says Dādū'.

12. Svāmiji replied: "He is our god,
by Whom all has been created.
We meditate on the Name of Hari and
controlling the senses we glorify Rām."

13. The Sheikh said: "Your god has no name and
no fixed place; in what village was he born?"
"You have spoken correctly", said Dādū,
and he gave a complete explanation to the Sheikh and the King:

14. "As I said, He has no name;
call Him *sāhib*, it makes you no wiser.
For our own satisfaction we give Him names,
according to the qualities we discover in Him.

15. Because He shows mercy, we call Him Dayāl,
because He protects creatures, we call Him Gopāl,
because He dwells in every heart, we call Him Rām,
because He is compassionate, we call Him Rahim.

16. Because He cannot be grasped, we call Him Allah,
because He cannot be described, we call Him Alakh,
because He created every thing, we call Him Sirjanhār,
because He is without end, we call Him Apār.

17. Because He can charm, we call Him Mohan,
because in all things He is the beauty, we call Him Vyāpi.
Did sugar ever announce it was sweet,
or did the *nim* tree proclaim its bitter essence?

18. In that way only can we meditate on His names.
He accepts the love and commitment of His devotees,
He honours their true service
His presence is manifest throughout the world."

19. The King and the Sheikh enjoyed this greatly,
as if that day they experienced the Almighty.

(60) See above, v. 1.13, note.

They took great pains to go and announce to the Emperor
that in Dādū they had found a real treasure:

20. "Such a saint has never appeared before
and shall never be seen again."
The Emperor gave instructions to bring Dādū,
as he was sincerely looking forward to seeing him.

21. The Sheikh and King Bhagvant Dās
escorted Dādū to Emperor Akbar.
"With Allah or Rām in your mind,
please come with us", they said.

22. The Emperor Akbar asked Dādū
where he was now living.
"I live where the Master instructs me to live,
I do not decide myself where to come or go.

23. In fact the Master brought me to your presence,
nothing that He orders fails."
He spoke further about Sāmbhar and Āmer,
where his King, his Highest Guru became manifest.

24. Akbar: "You live so close by,
messages could easily come and go.
When you find a real treasure,
you must distribute and share it.

25. Whatever desire is in your heart,
allow me to fulfill it."
Svāmījī replied: "I really do not lack anything.
What can you do with water, if you are not thirsty?"

26. The Emperor then asked him to give a lecture,
but Svāmījī suggested he should ask questions.
After some time had passed
Svāmījī recited a couplet[61]:

> 1. "Did water come first or first the light,
> did earth come first or first the heavens,
> was the anvil first or first the hammer,
> what is the explanation about man and woman?
> 2. Whoever can answer,
> he will be my teacher".
> Svāmījī reflected and said:
> "Only the Able One can give an answer.
> 3. 'With a single word He created everything,
> so powerful is He.
> Only weak humans think
> in terms of causality[62]'.
> 4. The body is a churn, the mind is the milk,
> the life-giver churns it.
> Kabīr took the essence, but
> worldly people drink the whey "
> 5. After some time had passed,
> Svāmījī recited a couplet.

(61) The couplet follows next in Mss. ACDG. Verses 26.1ff are clearly interpolated in Mss. BEF: they are questions to which again verse 27 gives the answer.

(62) *Dādūvāṇī*, Caturvedī ed., v. 22.8.

27. "The body is a churn, the mind is the milk,
The life-giver[63] churns it.
Kabir took the essence,
To support others."

1. '*Dādū:* With a beakful of water
a bird cannot empty the ocean.
No vessel has been made
to contain the whole ocean.'[64]
2. With folded hands Akbar bowed his head:
"Never have I heard such a reply.
I questioned him on the six systems
and nobody ever gave me such an answer".

28. Thus the Emperor conversed with Dādū Dīndayāl.
If you hear this story, you'll delight in it,
says Jan Gopāl.

chapter 6

1. Akbar asked Dādū to explain
how he could find the treasure.
Svāmījī dispelled his doubts and
Akbar knew he had found the treasure[65].

2. "How can one attain this state of mind?
Nothing is hidden from the saints,
please explain what one has to do and
show everyone the right way"[66].

3. 'The soul, filled with passionate yearning,
stands expectant at the door of vision.
The surrendered heart is always present before the divine,
watchful and alert, *Dādū*.'[67]

4. "First destroy the physical desires,
which tie you to worldly passions.
Give up all hopes in the three worlds,
and surely Brahma will reveal His light."

5. King Bīrbal and Tursī asked the Emperor
to try to understand what Dādū was getting at:
"Only if you give up attachments to the world, the body
and the mind, can you experience the nectar of Rām".

6. "He said very well to give up attachments to body and mind,
but he never possessed anything of the three worlds.
Brother, go and try to have a house of your own,
and then go and preach detachment to others."

7. Svāmījī said: "Let me explain to you
how I came to abandon all worldly attachments.

(63) *Prān*, lit.: 'life-breath' or God.
(64) *Dādūvāṇī*, Caturvedī ed., v. 4.304.
(65) For *vastu*, see above, v.3.22.1, note.
(66) *Mārg*, synonymous of *rāh*, lit.: 'path'.
(67) *Dādūvāṇī*, Caturvedī ed., v. 3.61.

The Creator made all living beings and
he gave to each one basically the same.

8. He gave a little food and some grains
to Kings and peasants alike.
People keep increasing their desires
and they amazingly never find fulfilment.

9. When a person has ten, he wants twenty,
when he has twenty he wants one hundred,
when he has a million, he wants a billion: as his
possessions increase, they look to him smaller and smaller.

10. First he thinks he should have the whole earth;
then he wants to take possession of the heavens,
of Indra, Shiva, Brahma and finally the world of death.
How can the Creator give all this?

11. When all these dreams have vanished,
you abandon all worldly desires, my friends".
"Wonderful, wonderful", said Akbar,
"I have never before heard such teachings".

12. Akbar said he was highly impressed and
invited him for more discussions and instructions.
Svāmiji replied he would not come back as
he wanted to go far away and meditate in solitude on the Name.

13. "Where then do you live?" Akbar asked.
"Wherever Rām wants me to be", said Svāmiji.
With this kind of conversation,
the Emperor was rather disturbed.

14. The Sheikh then proposed to take Dādū to his residence and
report to the Emperor any serious news.
King Birbal supported that proposal and
Emperor Akbar agreed to it.

15. "He can be my guest for a couple of days and
I shall inform the Emperor if discussions are to be held".
Akbar gave instructions to give Dādū all comfort and
come to him if anything was lacking.

16. Emperor Akbar went back to his quarters and
Svāmiji was escorted by King Birbal.
The King told him: "O joygiver,
you and I are the friends of Gobinda".

17. As they proceeded Svāmiji continued his instruction and
the King held him by the hand.
He took[68] him to his own palace and gave him rooms
close to the main gate.

18. After a couple of days the King spoke unkindly
and hurt Svāmiji's feelings.
"Really Akbar felt quite unhappy,
when you did not comply with his request".

(68) The verb *ṭhilānā* lit. means: 'to take one forcefully to... .

19. To Svāmiji's question 'Who is pleased with the truth?',
the King replied: "The Lord of the world".
"Then", said Dādū, "if He is pleased with my statement,
let people take it well or ill".

20. The King pointed out that the Emperor is God incarnate *(avatār)*,
and that even Dādū should give him respect:
"He is looked at with great respect and worshipped
as a God by both Hindus and Muslims".

21. Svāmiji replied: "I worship only One
and do not bow to any other.
All created beings are in the power of death,
only Brahmā does not come or go".

22. The King said: "Whoever that is,
in your view He is different.
We serve him who acknowledges service.
If that is (the Emperor), please forgive me."

23. The King put many penetrating questions
and could not find fault in Svāmiji's teaching.
So from that day he worshipped Rām
and all his doubts disappeared.

24. The disciple Cāndā was brave
and totally committed to service.
Even when Svāmiji tried to frighten him,
no fear could enter his heart.

25. The King escorted Dādū to the quarters of his wives,
who were very happy when they saw him.
Dādū was shown the temples, palaces and residences,
but he showed not the slightest interest.

26. When they entered the palace of mirrors,
Svāmiji exclaimed it was all unreal.
"If that is unreal, I'll give it all up
and become your disciple", said the King.

27. Svāmiji replied: "Just remember it is not real,
do good to others and that is your asceticism".
Svāmiji returned to his quarters
and reports were sent to the Emperor.

28. Meeting Dādū Dindayāl, is like drinking nectar.
Everyone should know of his conversations
with King Birbal, described by Jan Gopāl.

chapter 7

1. The discussions lasted for 40 days[69],
there seemed to be no end to it.
Dādū spoke with the firmness of Prahlād
and with the wisdom of Kabir.

(69) If *cārisā* is only to rhyme with *bisā*, it should be understood as *cāri*, 'four'.

2. He radiated the contemplative mind of Sukhdev[70]
and had the ascetic appearance of Gorakhnāth.
Illusions and attachments did not distress or bother him,
when you looked at him, he was all bliss.

3. The Emperor wondered what should be done
and asked the King for his opinion.
The King said: "If you can go and see him now,
greet him with folded hands and head bent.

4. Please him with your humble speech,
ask for his blessing[71] and take his hand on your head.
The blessing of a saint gives a vision of Khudā,
without a blessing disaster will befall you."

5. Akbar ordered: "Bring Dādū quickly,
if he does not mind meeting me".
The King went to his palace.
No one knew how Svāmījī would react.

6. A nobleman was sent to invite Dādū,
who appeared to live close to the King's palace:
"If you wish, the King will come and see you,
or if you come to his palace, he can see you there."

7. Svāmījī decided to go along immediately,
and took his disciple Jan Gopāl with him.
Jagjīvan was asked to stay back,
while Svāmījī went to see the King.

8. The King came to meet him and said:
"May the Almighty always keep me in your shelter.
I wish to inform you of the Emperor's desire
to see you again, o joygiver".

9. The King accompanied Dādū to the imperial court,
where they were at once received by the Emperor.
When the King had announced that Dādū was present,
the discussions with the Emperor started.

10. Svāmījī did not express any greeting;
he remained indifferent, avoiding all involvement.
"Tell me about the Gosvāmī", said Akbar,
"tell me how to discern milk from water".

11. Svāmījī replied: "If the body is not pure,
how can one appreciate about Gosvāmī[72]?"
"If I wasn't sure you had experienced Gosvāmī,
I wouldn't have invited you here", said Akbar.

12. "Working hard day and night,
there are plenty of cotton-carders in Sīkrī"[73].
Svāmījī replied: "It is all a matter of luck,
if you see the way people get around.

(70) See above, v.1.3, note.
(71) *Davā* is here understood as *duā*, 'mercy, blessing'.
(72) With such a line Jan Gopāl clearly underlines the superiority of Dādū, who dares to suggest that the Emperor is a 'sinner'. See also above 6.21 and 7.10.
(73) In Mss. BEF we read: 'Roaming around in a holy dress, there are many beggars in Sīkrī'.

13. All sorts of people have come in the world,
how many of them have found Gosvāmī?"
Emperor Akbar asked Svāmījī
to explain that mystery:

14. "My mind is so involved in worldly affairs,
how can I experience the Creator?
With my whole being[74]
I want to commit myself to the path you prescribe.

15. I shall infuse my heart with truth,
if in that way I may find Gosvāmī".
"Wonderful", said Svāmījī,
"may Gosvāmī always keep you to this resolve.

16. If you listen to what I say,
Gosvāmī will always give you this attitude".
Emperor Akbar bowed his head:
"You have given and I have received".

1. Dādū, the beloved of our heart,
gave a blessing to the ruler of Delhi:
"May the Master always keep you
in prosperity and kindness".

17. Akbar then begged him
to take whatever he liked as a gift.
But Svāmījī replied he could use nothing,
except for the love of the Almighty.

18. Akbar said: "Please take whatever you like,
so you can worship, eat and give to eat".
Svāmījī: "True worship consists
of serving day and night".

19. Akbar: "How can you support yourself?
You should accept gifts if you do not work".
"We all have a job
and share our food with the devotees".

20. 'I am the servant of the Able One,
I am never without work, *Kabir*.
The husband gets the blame,
if his wife is clothed in rags[75]'.

21. Akbar: "Take gold, silver or clothes,
whatever I give you is too little.
Villages or districts, horses and elephants,
I give them as a mark of my praise"[76].

(74) Lit.: 'with all the hairs on my body'.
(75) *Kabīr-Granthāvalī*, Tivārī ed., 11.8 (Vaudeville:1974, p. 213).
(76) Lit.: 'as a companion to my praise'.
After this line, an additional interesting line is found only in Mss. AC (which give the early version):
'If you are addicted to the nectar of Rām,
No other drink will tempt you' (lit.: 'sherbet is not sweet').

22. "Clothed in rags and hungry,
the ascetic only gathers the richess of Hari.
The Emperor should leave his empire and
leaving his throne the King should sit on the ground.

23. Staying away from gold and women,
one enters the presence of the Master.
As long as an ascetic keeps touching wealth,
he commits a grave sin".

1. 'For your sake, Master,
I have given up the city of Bulkh[77],
with 16 thousand women
and 1,8 million horses'.

24. Akbar: "I am aware of all this, but
accept and distribute these and I'll be happy".
Svāmījī: "I would like this as your present
that you treat all beings impartially".

25. 'Let no being suffer
and the Creator will be pleased.
Stay always in the presence of the Master,
give alms and encourage others to do the same'.

1. From that moment Akbar stopped hurting living beings,
since he had found Dādū, the excellent *pir*.
He made his decision into a religious law,
that no one should hurt living beings[78].
2. Akbar's attitude of mercy
did not suit the Qāzīs and the Mullās.
They all agreed they should try
to reduce Dādū's power.
3. They prayed to the Prophet:
"Beloved, please take note of that power.
You have helped us with clear instructions;
please perform a miracle for us".
4. Akbar had a throne prepared
on which no other person was allowed to sit.
He was eager to see with whom real power was.
'Who knows the ways of the Unknowable?'
5. The throne was nicely arranged and
king Bīrbal was sent to Svāmījī.
The King invited Dādū,
who already 'knew' what was happening.
6. "Why have you come", Svāmījī asked.
"I was sent to invite you", the King replied.
Svāmījī saw his inner thoughts
and disclosed what was being planned.
7. Abdul Fazl and King Bīrbal stared at
Svāmījī, in wonder.
He said: "You may go and say
that I am coming; do not worry".
8. Svāmījī then became the embodiment of love[79] and took his disciple Jaggā with him.

(77) Bulkh was supposed to be a fabulous city.

(78) This is clearly a later addition. The injuction not to harm living beings does not follow logically from Dādū's earlier statements in this context.

(79) For the various meanings of *surati* in Sant literature, see Callewaert:1978, p. 339.

Via a secret road he went to the Emperor,
who was greatly astonished at what he saw.
9. A strange[80] throne appeared in the sky,
radiating bright light and splendid beauty.
Svāmījī sat on it, like
the Highest-above-all, the Indweller.
10. Akbar was terrified:
Who can know the ways of Dādū?
The Emperor came down from his throne, bowing low:
"You are the Master, I am your slave".
11. With this miraculous display,
the ignorance[81] of the Emperor disappeared:
"I am satisfied, God has appeared,
my doubts[82] have gone".

26. Be contented, your head bowed in humility,
fully concentrated on the Compassionate,
as the goldsmith only thinks of precious stones
and the jeweller knows even the smallest stone.

27. Emperor Akbar is very intelligent,
discerning good from evil.
Svāmījī took his leave and went away,
but the King kept asking him (to stay).

28. Hear how Dādū Dīndayāl gave up *māyā*.
Give up everything yourself, if you want to,
says Jan Gopāl.

chapter 8

1. "As Emperor Akbar has suggested,
please stay a few days more", said the King.
Svāmījī: "If that will please you,
it is all right with me".

2. Svāmījī then went with the King
and the disciples were informed.
The next morning King Bīrbal
invited Svāmījī to this residence.

3. The rooms, full of beautiful carpets,
enchanted even gods, not only humans.
The King offered him a chair to sit on,
knowing that the place where Svāmījī enters is blessed.

4. In the night where Svāmījī is the moon,
where knights and Kings are the stars,
the famous hymns are the light of the world!
The King implored the joygiver to teach him.

5. The King mixed all kinds of coins
and filled a bag with them.

(80) *Adhar*, lit. 'which cannot be grasped'; this term is also used as an epithet for God.

(81) Lit.: 'the darkness'.

(82) Lit.: 'my suffering'.

He added different kinds of jewelry
and distributed it among the disciples and Nāga soldiers.

6. As the King put the gifts at Svāmījī's feet,
Dādū showed great indifference:
"If you want to please me, remember
I only take to give, I do not receive.

7. It is the empty vessel you must fill with water,
if the vessel is already full more water will spill out.
Except for Hari, there is no room in my mind,
What use do I have for your coins?"

8. The King: "Please accept these and
if you like, give them to the poor".
Svāmījī: "To whom does this *māyā* belong and
Who is the King of the poor?

9. The Lord fills the whole universe,
whatever we see is perfect.
The King: "My gifts are like ritual left-overs[83],
I offer them to you, please keep them.

10. I give them to you with my own hands".
Svāmījī: "You offered them to the Lord of the universe".
The King called Brahmans and bards,
all kinds of poor came together.

11. Svāmījī gave instructions to give to all,
but a Brahman showed dissatisfaction:
"Hail to the King", he complained, "but
king Bīrbal has not given what I asked for"[84].

12. The King: "I offered my wealth and my houses,
and still it does not tempt Svāmījī".
Blessed is Svāmījī, who gave up all *māyā*,
he is the greatest ascetic of the Kali age.

1. When Svāmījī saw King Bīrbal's insight,
he commented:
"Everyone can recognize a clear mind, but
you need special discernment to recognize the Master".
2. King Bīrbal clearly showed his humility,
he took off his turban and put it at Svāmījī's feet:
"You make me feel very shy,
I can't possibly approach Gosvāmī."
3. Svāmījī felt pity for him and
placed the turban on his own head, upside down:
"I load the three worlds on my head
and the Creator will take away your shyness".
4. 'You may meet a *siddha* and yet not find right insight[85].
If you meet a brave *siddha*, all your troubles disappear'.
5. Gorakh Nāth walked down a lane
and was given abundant grace.
Humility pleases God;
should He redeem a sinner?

(83) *Nirmālay* (Skt. *nirmālya*) refers to the flowers that have been offered to the deity in a temple.

(84) The meaning of this line is not certain.

(85) The meaning of the line is not clear.

6. Svāmījī showed mercy on Bīrbal and
gave him the spirit of real devotion.

13. Reflect on this: there is nothing
a man's Kingdom or family can do in his place.
Then Svāmījī got up and walked away,
but the King came running after him.

14. The King was greatly moved, half choked
with emotion, weeping with love.
"When can I sit with you again,
when do I again have the honour of seeing you?"

1. "If you can stay close to us, Svāmījī,
we shall be very happy".
"You have been in my mind very often, Svāmījī,
for you are really a man of Hari.
2. Whenever I met a saint before,
there was always some business involved.
You really performed a miracle, Svāmījī,
attracting Akbar's mind to Hari".

15. King Bhavant Dās told him:
"It is wonderful you have come,
I have been worrying day and night,
hoping that Hari would protect you.

16. If only you could stay a little while,
I would be very pleased."

1. The King ordered plenty of gifts,
although Svāmījī said he was not interested.
The King: "My gifts are like ritual left-overs[86],
I offer them to you, please keep them.
2. Please accept my gifts;
offering to you, I offer them to Murārī."
Svāmījī: "Take my advice and
give the presents to the poor".
3. The King obeyed the order and distributed all.
For the sake of Svāmījī, wealth was shared.
The King made the ritual ambulation,
saying that the religion of Svāmījī was blessed.

Svāmījī left the town and
saints from all around came to see him.

17. Wherever Svāmījī came,
saints of various sects sang his praise.
With his seven co-travellers he stayed in the jungle,
avoiding the villages for fear of the crowds.

1. They sat down near a pond and
Svāmījī instructed his disciples to take a bath.
Sitting near the stream, Jaggā wished
they had some hot *jalebī* sweets to eat.
2. When he saw his disciples hungry,
Svāmījī miraculously ordered a plate.

(86) See above, v.8.9. Exactly the same lines are found in the context of king Birbal, in Mss BEF.

The food the disciples had asked for,
came floating on the water.
3. Where can you meet a real guru,
better than Dādū Dīndayāl?
He turned a desolate forest
into a pleasant place for festivities.

18. In Aulaudā lived Lākhā Narhar and
the devotee Damodar, who had given up all worldly concerns.
From Dyausā Dādū was taken all around
and great devotion was shown to him.

19. He finally arrived in Āmer,
where the followers experienced great joy.
If Rām takes care of some one,
nobody can disturb him.

1. A *yogī* sat on a rock and made it float,
relying on the promise of the King of fishes.
Dādū's disciple Ṭīlā spoke out and
made the rock fly in the air.
2. Ṭīlā then felt pity and
made the rock and the *yogī* come down again.
The *yogī* fell at his feet,
and begged to be made Dādū's disciple.
3. Svāmījī too took pity and
made the *yogī* his disciple.
Growing in love the *yogī* lived with Dādū and
was called his disciple.

20. A Muslim came and brought some cooked meat,
hiding it in a piece of cloth.
When he opened it there was sugar and rice instead,
and he knew Dādū was a great saint.

21. Fearing shipwreck on a river,
a businessman remembered Dādū's deeds:
"Dādū, Dādū", he called,
"please save my life.

22. I shall offer half my stock to God
and forever remember your name."
The boat touched the bank safely
and the stock was offered for the sake of Dādū.

23. "Ascetics do not eat sweet crumbled bread":
this news came ahead of him to Amer.
Everyone knows the events that occurred in Devnagar,
these glorious events Jan Gopāl relates.

1. Seven hundred merchants sat in their ships,
carrying goods worth millions.
While crossing[87], the ships got stuck in the river.
2. In the Ḍhūṇḍhār region King Mān
had helped to promote the *bhakti* of Rām.
Rajab: the merchants called the Name,
and the ships could move again.
3. One day, in the Himalayas,
king Bīrbal was caught in an avalanche.

(87) The meaning of the line is not clear.

It happened in a valley of Kashmir,
where one should not make noise.
4. Not giving attention, the King had shouted,
and the snow came down with deafening noise.
Remembering his promise, Dādū
rescued him without delay.
5. Earlier, King Birbal had put his head on Dādū's feet,
and had asked for total protection.
'If anyone seeks Dādū's protection,
he will not fail to find the ultimate state'.
6. One day, Dādū's subtle body[88] travelled,
witnessing an infinite variety of worlds.
A divine voice sounded, and resounded
as if having no end:
7. 'Beyond Beginning and End,
there is the Unparallelled Reality[89]
without form,
existing in itself, faultless:
no one knows its secret'.
8. 'Indestructible, without beginning or end,
untouched by suffering.
See and serve Him in your heart, *Dādū*.
Only very few know His secret'.

24. The immense qualities of Dādū are known all over.

chapter 9[1]

1. Who understands the tricks of a street magician,
who can explain the ways of the Creator?

1. As Kamāl was born to Kabīr,
so too did Dādū have children.
2. He gave (to his wife) two cloves and two pepper-corns.
The ways of Svāmī[2] are not known.
A real miracle happened:
she became pregnant and four children were born.

How were Svāmiji's children born,
through gift or in the human way[3]?

2. In Sāmbhar, when he was thirty two, during the rainy season[4],
the Lord of the world had given him children.

(88) *Surati*, lit. 'love'. See above, ch. 7.8, note.
(89) *Anūpam dev*.

(1) This chapter 9 is numbered 10 in Mss. A and D, in which the order of chapters 9 and 10 is inverted. Somehow, this chapter locks out of place. It does not fit chronologically. After the meeting with Akbar in 1585, we read now that Garib Dās was born in 1575. Chapter 10 seems to continue the story of chapter 8. Is chapter 9 a later addition or an oral account inserted by Jangopāl?
(2) *Svāmi* stands both for Dādūji and for God.
(3) The -very controversial- second half of the couplet is missing in Mss. BEF and in the Sukh Dayāl Dādū edition!
(4) *Shrāvan* corresponds to 15 July - 15 August.

Dādū was with us as a father,
the first son born to him was Garib Dās.

3. As the child grew up corresponding to his age,
he acquired full wisdom[5],
like Nārad playing the flute,
like Gandharvas singing loudly,

4. like Tumbar[6] clapping his hands for rhythm,
with a nectar-like voice and sweet speech:
enumerate all the talents in the world,
Garib Dās was endowed with them.

5. An ascetic from birth, totally detached as a youth,
wise Garib Dās knew no passion.
Jangopāl sings his praise and
tells you about Dādū's other children.

6. The second son is Maskin,
who was all the time immersed in Rām.
He served Svāmiji constantly,
developing intense feelings of devotion.

1. Faithfully obeying Svāmiji,
feelings of devotion swelled in his heart.
Full of love and contemplation of Hari,
Maskin was always in ecstasy.

2. Totally committed to the remembrance of Hari,
all day and all night in ecstasy,
ignorant of the ways of the world,
meditating on the Undivided, the Unstained.

7. Besides his two sons, Dādū had
two daughters: Havā and the ascetic Bāi.
For his wife Nāni and the two daughters,
Jangopāl is singing praises.

8. Sant Dās the Gujarāti requested Sāngā
to take good care of Rāmdās.
In the temple of Bairsal lived the old Dayāl Dās,
a faithful devotee of Hari.

9. The Kāyastha fellow-devotees
escorted Svāmiji to that temple.
He gave them great joy
and they sang his praises enthusiastically[7].

10. Flocking together people sang the praises of Rām.
Finally, Svāmiji arrived in Āmer and then,
after one year the time came again
to start travelling about.

(5) Lit.: "At five, seven, ten, twelve years of age,
he became acquainted with everything".

(6) Tumburu is the Gandharva son of Nārad and expert in divine music. He is known in the Purāṇas for having sung the glories of Ananta and having praised Hiranyakaśipu.

(7) Lit: 'for all ages'.

11. In Tonk Narhar Dās and Mādhav Kāṇi,
organized a very popular festival.
Only after great insistence they could invite Svāmījī,
and there was no end to the number of saints present.

12. The Andhiyā garden was like a *bāzār*,
crowds lined up to see Dādū.
To the beat of drums they sang his praises,
everybody was able to see Dādū.

1. Realizing food-supplies were getting short,
Mādhav Kāṇi informed Svāmījī,
who replied: "Do not worry,
know that the Indweller is present".
2. Plates full of food were brought
and Svāmījī distributed the meals of Hari.
Sacred offerings were collected in vessels,
and the saints witnessed the endless supply.
3. Eventually Ṭīlā pointed out to Svāmījī
that the sacred offerings were running out.
The thoughtful teacher Dādū
made the offerings again to arrive in plentiful.
4. "What[8] is this trick of Svāmījī?",
Ṭīlā asked the Indweller.
Knowing that people have external eyes only,
the Creator turns their understanding inside out.
5. In the play of King Rām
all saints participate.
Becoming one with the Self,
all wrong conceptions disappear.
6. The Eternal, Supreme Brahma appeared,
everyone longed for the sacred offerings.
Svāmījī saw their devotion[9].
7. The merciful Svāmī was moved by mercy and
gave cloves, to everybody's satisfaction.
Is there anything the Able One cannot do?
No one knows the ways of the Unknown.
8. Mādhav, who was in charge, asked: "Generous one,
you are good to all beings.
Now you have asked only for four cloves,
how will you satisfy everyone?"
9. The Indweller distributed in accordance
with the depth of each person's feelings:
some were given five, six or seven cloves,
Mādhav witnessed that everyone was given.
10. All doubts disappeared and
the Sants experienced deep satisfaction.
The festivities at Tonk
made Dādū immensely famous.
11. 'When touched by the Beloved,
the body becomes all love.
Uniting mind and body,
that is true remembrance, *Dādū*'[10].

13. The festival went on for seven days,
then Svāmījī took leave and went away.

(8) This verse is found only in Ms. F.
(9) The meaning of the complete line is not certain.
(10) *Dādūvāṇī*, Caturvedī ed., v. 4.150.

He made his entry in Guḍhalā,
in the company of young disciples.

14. On the road they were surrounded by singers, and
with great kindness Svāmījī was watching them.
In great numbers the singers
just stood there and Svāmījī enjoyed it greatly.

15. As he made his way the singers came along
and when he stopped they bent their heads.
The saints were highly amazed,
but Svāmījī directed their eyes to Hari.

1. Dādū the merciful
showed compassion when he came.
Jangopāl has no doubt:
all the singers found liberation.

16. Like an experienced actor Dādū came to Guḍhalā,
where the devotee Damodar experienced great joy.
For three days there were fascinating meetings
and deep feelings of devotion were shared.

17. Svāmījī then returned to Āmer
and made it clear he would not travel again.
After a couple of days, however,
the disciples came with a new request:

18. "Please Svāmījī, come to us
and bring our works to fulfilment.
Pūrn Dās was a merchant in Āndhī,
leaving wordly attachments he was immersed in Rām".

19. Svāmījī frequently came there and
religious celebrations were arranged, with songs of praise.
The *yogī* Jaimal of Sāmbhar
was a joyful disciple of Svāmījī.

20. When Svāmījī came to his house,
his brother Chājū bent to the ground before him.
Haridās, Rānā and Mohan
were all companion disciples of Jaimal.

21. Svāmījī came and gave them joy,
Greatly pleasing all disciples.
There was the remarkable Kapil of Chātsū,
a mystic who knew the world to be shallow.

22. Svāmījī's disciples liked him very much
and arranged celebrations in order to invite him.
Svāmījī gave them great joy, and
people everywhere sang his praises.

23. Tolhā and Bāgar came and joined him,
not caring for people's praise or scorn.
They concentrated on the Almighty, while
both Hindus and Muslims disliked this.

24. In Āmer lived the ascetic
disciple Lāldās, with an alert mind,

and Cetan, Keśav, Baghu and Dūjan,
who highly respected the dust on Svāmījī's feet.

25. There was the ascetic Mohan Dās of Pattan,
fully detached of *māyā*.
He came with the chieftain Lāl Dās
and was able to see Svāmījī.

26. Further also Prāgdās, Jhājhū and Bhagvān,
the talented Haridās and Gopāl,
the good-natured Mohan Dās of Mevār,
all disciples of Svāmījī, endowed with virtues.

27. The life-story of Dādū the merciful
is endless, illimited.
Jangopāl keeps narrating it,
day and night.

chapter 10

1. When many days had passed,
the Creator undertook to make his fame immortal[11].
King Mānsingh[12] made his entry in Āmer
and large crowds came to see him.

2. The King came to Manoharpur, Acalor
and Rāmgarh which is close by.
Everyone met him at his residence, with great respect:
only Svāmījī stayed at home.

3. After a couple of days,
people started to slander Svāmījī:
"Dādū has deeply offended you, o King,
he has not given you due respect.

4. In fact, he offends others too in this way".
The King was interested to know how, (and they said:)
"He proclaims that Hindus and Muslims are one,
that Brahmans and Baniyās[13] are equal.

5. Where is the distinction between the four castes?
The Vedas are proclaimed false,
deceased women are left behind in the jungle
without ritual, they are not even buried.

6. No religion is safe anymore,
both Hindus and Muslims are going astray.
Our children are encouraged to remain celibate,
while the Vedas are said to be erroneous.

7. Till the age of 7 you call a girl *kanyā*,
till the age of 12 she is called *beṭī*.

(11) In Mss. BEF we read: 'Bhagvant Singh was immersed in Hari'.
(12) See above, 4.8n.
(13) Baniyās are merchants, usually of the third caste.

(If unmarried) at the age of 16, it is bad[14],
at the age of 20, it is unpardonable[15].

8. Disorder is brought to our land,
who can justify such action?".
The King then decided to go and meet Svāmījī,
with all affection, and discuss these matters.

9. He mentioned he had not forgotten that
he had met Dādū at Rāmgarh some years before:
"I have seen your quest, Svāmījī,
but you never came to inquire about me here".

10. "I did inquire about essentials", was Dādū's answer,
"whenever the Almighty suggested it to me".
The King asked for an explanation of
the custom to leave the corpses to Rām:

11. "Do you bury or burn the corpses?"
Svāmījī replied with a couplet:
'The brave ascetic enhances the open field,
He knows no tomb or cremation-ground'.

12. '*Kabīr*, one should retire to die in a place
where no one is available,
where people eat animal flesh:
nobody understands this'.[16]

13. 'Remembering Hari, life is successful,
if spent in the service of others.
There one should die, says Dādū,
Where birds and beasts can feed on you'.[17]

14. The King thought of the celibacy of children,
but did not know how to approach the question.
Svāmījī understood what the King had in mind,
a great person discerns inner thoughts.

15. He said: "One should not impose marriage
on young persons who will get the blame[18].
Parents have little intelligence,
they make terrible mistakes.

1. If so many people burn with lust and passion,
there can be no wrong in continence".
The King got very frightened,
for Svāmījī seemed to read everybody's mind.

2. 'The relationship of man and woman is hell
if only based on lust, says Kabīr.
It is a path to Rām,

(14) Lit.: 'it is against *dharma*'.
(15) Lit.: 'it produces bad *karma*'.
(16) The reading of the last line is different in the Tivāri edition, with the following translation in Vaudeville:1974 (p. 264): 'and nobody invokes the Name'.
(17) *Dādūvāṇi*, Caturvedi ed., v. 2.44.
(18) This refers to child-marriage which may result in early widowhood. Interestingly, *instead* of this line, we read in Mss. BEF:
"Svāmījī removed all doubts. The King listened quietly, with folded hands'.

if you can meditate without passion'.[19]

16. "We are sisters and brothers of Rām,
otherwise all relations turn adulterous.
Is there any wisdom in joining two pots?
Touch one clay pot with another and they break!

17. A man and a woman embrace each other,
they think of nothing else and
forget Hari completely:
in that sense marriage is meaningless.

18. Brahmans and Baniyās are powerful Kings,
at the age of seven their daughters become widows.

1. If they take off in pursuit of passion,
on whom must the blame be laid?

Why should they forever face the scorn of the world,
this is no work of the Almighty."

They have abortions
to avoid disgrace.
2. Give your undivided attention only to Brahmā,
He is the Judge of good and truth.

19. Everyone said: "Wonderful, wonderful,
who can be blamed for such ideas?"
Svāmījī continued: "I do not impose or forbid marriage,
each individual should choose the nectar or the poison."

20. 'He is mother, mother-in-law and wife.
Give attention, Sants; I have reached the ultimate, *Kabīr.*'

21. 'Every man and woman is your brother and sister,
all are children of the Almighty, says Dādū'.[20]

22. The King was pleased with the answers of Svāmījī,
and the disciples present went around telling everyone.
The King said: "It doesn't seem to matter to you,
what kind of person becomes your disciple"[21].

23. Svāmījī: "I do not make disciples,
people come on their own, immersed (in God),
like the lotus recognizing the moon,
or the snake smelling the sandaltree.

24. Like the lotus awakening to the sun
or the moth attracted to a lamp.
A boat does not have to be shouted at:
it takes across all who get into it.

(19) *Kabīr-Granthāvalī*, Tivārī ed., v. 30.5. Vaudeville:1974 (p. 296) translates the second line in a different way: *'Those men belong to Rām,* who invoke Him free from desire'.
I propose my translation on the assumption that the first line suggests: 'it need not be a hell if *not* based on lust'.

(20) *Dādūvāṇī*, Caturvedī ed., v.12.114.

(21) This remark implies that Dādū receives both Hindus and Muslims and persons of all castes.

25. Sants come from everywhere,
king Rām takes care of all of them.
Lovely hue is produced when lime and *haldi* are mixed,
like the meeting of two people in love".

26. "How do you provide all the food,
if you accept no dowry and earn no money?
Clothes are beautiful on a tall person
and you have many persons in your company."

27. 'If alive you are like dead,
and give up all worldly hopes, says Kabir,
then Hari himself goes to serve you
and the disciple knows no sorrow'.[22]

28. This was the conversation of Dādū and the King.
If you do not know it, you will not find divine taste,
says Jangopāl.

chapter 11

1. During the discussions with King Mānsingh,
the disciple Ṭīlā was the spokesman.
He gave competent answers in the discussion,
trying to avoid an uprising.

    1. The answers of Tīlā were such that
    king Mānsingh remained speechless.
    He understood, after some reflection,
    that all is empty without the Name of Rām.

2. Seeing that the King was favourable (to Dādū),
the Brahmans felt badly humiliated.
Asked why they appeared so abashed,
they replied that Dādū was a real nuisance to them.

3. "People go to him and call on Rām,
nobody comes to our Hindu rituals[23].
If your majesty goes on to support Dādū,
everyone will join his sect".

4. The King considered this carefully:
"The Creator is far away from me:
If a saint has given up all desires[24],
nothing can be an obstacle to him".

    1. "If I spoil my relation with the Brahmans,
    my royal affairs may be doomed.
    But if I harm a saint,
    I'll be disgraced and go to hell".

5. The King faced an awful dilemma:
"This saint is great, should he go or stay?"
He considered the period of stay and
asked how long Dādū had lived in Āmer.

(22) *Kabir-Granthāvali*, Tivāri ed., v. 19.11 (Vaudeville:1974,p. 259).
(23) *Bed* (or Vedas) stands here for the Hindu rituals organized by the Brahmans.
(24) Lit.: 'the body and the world'.

6. "For fourteen years now," Svāmījī replied,
"the Creator has given me protection".
Dādū got up to go. The King understood
he had offended the saint and was very embarrassed.

1. "I did not suggest you should get up,
I only asked a straight question.
It was a great offense, please forgive me,
I know you are of the Indweller."

7. Svāmījī reassured him: "Do not be afraid, King,
through you Rām has spoken to me.
Hari is the intermediary between you and me,
there is no question here of good or bad statements."

8. "You are indeed a great saint,
why do I repeat the words of evil people?"

1. When Svāmījī decided to get up,
The Almighty was very angry.
A voice was heard from heaven:
'Dādū's word will bring about destruction'.
2. Svāmījī, however, showed great compassion
and Hari liberated all beings.
3. Beings are like orphans and
the Creator saves them all.
If you pray to Rām,
nobody will be destroyed.
4. Nārad is furious without the Sants,
his fury is expressed in one word.
A town is saved when protected by a saint,
unharmed by lightning or rocks.
5. If the Master is angry,
He can totally destroy it.
Svāmījī then prayed to Hari,
who had protected him in Āmer.
6. The King acted like a servant
and touched Svāmījī's feet.
"Now I do not let you go,
please stay, for the mercy of Indweller"
7. When Mānsingh bent down his head,
Dādū made him, the lord of the world, his disciple.
He built a temple near the bank of the lake,
and close to the water a garden was made.
8. Thus the King was very satisfied and
asked Svāmījī to stay a few more days.
Svāmījī had patience with the King,
but kept going round begging for alms.

He came home and distributed everything,
clothes and food, all was given away.

9. The ascetic Svāmījī started on his wanderings, and
with firm mind his disciples accompanied him.
For about five days they were on the road, and
with his fortunate disciples he halted in Bhurbhurā.

10. They were the guests of Rāghav Dās and
stayed there for three months.
In Kalyānpur lived a certain Pīthā,
a dedicated devotee, experienced in divine love.

11. He attended all celebrations, lived like an ascetic,
and stayed awake to be with Svāmiji.
He had been to Bhurbhurā to see Svāmiji
and there he found all his desires fulfilled.

12. He was very courageous in his devotion
and did not bother about the comments of people.
Svāmiji then came to Kalyānpur, people heard it and
were very happy in Hari Rām.

13. There he stayed for one year and left again,
going westward for a couple of days.
As if playing and sporting he arrived in Pādū,
where his disciple Takū served him.

14. Mādhav Dās invited him to Khandāyā,
where Mohan of Reyān came to meet him.
With the singing of hymns and the sight of Svāmiji,
Mādhav Dās reached the ecstasy of love.

15. A certain Narbad lived in Īḍvā.
He had left a royal post and sang the praise of the Blessed.
When he saw Svāmiji,
he showed great devotion and his love increased.

16. You should also know Kisansingh of Rāthor,
who became an accomplished disciple.
Svāmiji came to Tilānā, where
celebrations were organized, to the great joy of people.

17. There was the cotton-carder Sant Dās of Rewat,
a good ascetic, loved by the Almighty.
He was experienced in devotion and love
and Svāmiji knew his love.

18. Rāghav Dās of Rāni village,
son of Ūdā, was a devotee of Hari.
He served with great devotion
and informed the local King informed about Dādū's movements.

19. The Kacchvāhā had given away seven villages,
to fulfill a vow to the Almighty.
The Rāthor noble Mānsingh of Bhavādi
became the truthful disciple of Svāmiji.

20. Rāghav Dās, by caste a Cauhān
of Tosin was an accomplished disciple.
The brothers Prithirāj and Lakhu
developed real love for Svāmiji.

21. He stayed in their house for a few days,
and they served him as if he were the Indweller.
The life-story of Dādū the merciful is endless, illimited.
Jangopāl keeps narrating it, for the Almighty and holy men.

chapter 12

1. The King of Bhuraṭiyā near Bikaner
heard that Svāmījī was in the area.
He invited him to come immediately from Khātū,
where Svāmījī had arrived.

2. He had to call Svāmījī again from Tosinā,
for nobody knew Svāmījī's plans.
"What is your sect, how do you live,
what do you do and what do you preach?"

3. "The Name of Rām is my sect,
my way of living is control of the senses,
for my deeds watch my disciples:
their goal is to be immersed in Rām."

4. "They do not recite any texts", remarked the King.
"Please have patience, my friend,
do not suggest they have no wisdom,
because they do not recite texts."

5. A mad elephant stood at the entrance of the house,
that had been made available for Dādū to stay.
Svāmījī went in the direction of the elephant,
although Garib Dās tried to stop him:

6. "This elephant has no understanding,
take another road back to the house".
"It does not matter if this elephant has no sense,
the Able One is my protector."

7. Garīb Dās showed great courage
and taking Rajab by the arm,
they came out together with Svāmījī.
The King saw this and was amazed.

8. The elephant stood motionless,
as if he was painted in a picture.
The ascetic Ṭīlā also came along,
and ran behind Svāmījī.

9. Then Durgā invited him to his home
and served the joygiver with devotion.
The next day the King called Svāmījī again
and inquired about the rosary and sectarian marks:

10. "Everyone tells me that
you carry a special rosary[25].
For your wooden rosary I'll give you one of gold,
I'll find happiness and serve you always".

11. "My sectarian mark", said Svāmījī,
is the rosary of the mind which the Guru gave.
You do not need a rosary of wood or gold,
if Rām-within is in your heart".

(25) *Sumiran*, lit.: 'meditation.'

12. 'The wooden rosary instructs you:
do not move me but turn your mind around, *Kabīr*'.

13. 'The Sadguru has given the rosary of the mind,
strung on the thread of regular breathing.
My hands are still but I move the beads day and night:
this is the highest meditation, *Dādū*'.[26]

14. The King requested him to stay in town
and to attract disciples to his monastery.
"To serve you I'll have a house built and
keep away crowds in order to be in your presence."

15. Svāmījī said he would think it over and
decide according to the wish of the Indweller.
He left the King and returned home
and told the disciples about the invitation.

16. They discussed the matter and concluded
that Sants should not be totally dependent on others.
A few days later the King called for him
and Svāmījī spoke his mind clearly:

17. "We will follow the life Rām appoints for us,
not concerned with the favours of Kings or people.
They call on you, showing enthusiasm,
but later on their moods change."

1. Svāmījī showed no interest in the happiness,
which may arise form royal splendour.
Anyone ascending a royal throne
is soon intoxicated by its splendour.

18. Svāmījī proceeded to Tosīnā
and the monastery. This brought joy to the disciples.
After two years had passed
he was invited to the Ḍhūḍhāhar region.

19. Wherever Svāmījī went, people experienced joy,
as he entered their temple.
After about one year,
Lād Khān joined him.

20. In Naulāsā lived Īshvar Kacchvāhā,
a brave disciple, strictly observing his vows.
He had given up sexual relations with his wife,
they lived together like brother and sister.

21. Then he went to Ghāṭvā,
where Lād Khān served him for a couple of days.
Celebrations of great devotion were held, and
then Svāmījī went on his way again.

22. He was accompanied by Prāg Dās,
a merchant who became an excellent disciple.
They went to Kardaulī and
on the way they visited Sāhipur.

(26) *Dādūvāṇī*, Caturvedi ed., v.1.67.

23. There was the trustworthy Sāh Tilok,
very eager to see Svāmījī.
He walked a mile to come and meet Svāmījī
and showed great devotion.

24. He arranged for plenty of food and
in the instructions and singing he found happiness.
Svāmījī left early in the morning, and
his disciples accompanied him.

1. It then occurred to Sāh Tilok,
that he had not had a divine experience,
but Svāmījī inspired his heart
and removed all his doubts.

25. Sāh Tilok was put in charge
of the equipment that had arrived the day before:
blankets, cots and shawls,
mattresses and carpets, all together.

26. Tilok came and picked up a shawl,
and he saw Svāmījī sitting there.
He exclaimed: "One Svāmījī is sitting here,
and another one is sitting there".

27. He saw Svāmījī inside and outside,
and knew his birth was successful.
He submitted to Svāmījī, saying:
" Your ways cannot be known".

1. Sāh Tilok gave a piece of cloth
and Svāmījī told him to tie it around his waist.
Svāmījī performed a miracle:
the piece of cloth could not be tied!
2. Sāh Tilok was full of awe,
realizing that Svāmījī knows everyone's heart.
When he had seen Dādū in two different places,
he had no more doubts.

28. Svāmījī: "I have only one body and
only your devotion can always be close to you."
Then Svāmījī came to Kirdauli,
giving joy to Prāgdās.

1. Do not test a true ascetic,
but serve with real faith.
Sāh Tilok did serve Svāmījī earnestly,
but never understood his ways.

29. The *līlā* of Dādū Dindayāl is endless, beyond understanding.
May I utter the name 'Dādū' for all ages to come.

chapter 13

1. Svāmījī had a liking for the devotee Gopāl Dās[27],
who had come to give him an invitation.

(27) *Dādū Caritāmrit*, pp. 806-807.

By caste a merchant, he was
a servant of Hari, living in Didvānā.

2. He showed great zeal in whatever he did,
pleasing everyone with his feelings of devotion.
From everywhere people flocked to see Dādū,
all worthy persons were able to see him.

3. Religious celebrations were held for five days.
Then Svāmījī left, taking leave of everybody[28],
in the company of Gopāl Jośī of Nāgaur
and Rām Dās-with-the-great-devotion.

4. In Rodhū Svāmījī went to stay with the merchant Sāran,
to increase his devotion for Hari.
In many ways he made the Sants happy and
then returned to the main monastery.

5. There he stayed for three months
and then returned to Mārwār.
Holy men came to touch his feet
and bathed in the river of mystical experience.

1. From Ajmer[29] came a Muslim ascetic
offering two presents.
In a leaf-plate he gave sugar-candy and flowers,
but Svāmījī accepted them only with reluctance.
2. When half an hour had passed
he asked for five cakes.
Dādū gave permission to leave and
the ascetic took his presents back with him (as cakes).
3. The Indweller knows everybody's mind and
Svāmījī does not keep other peoples' gifts.
Whatever was given to him he gave away,
saying that he possessed a hidden treasure.
4. The Sants said they did not understand the Indweller,
but Svāmījī replied: "I do not want any worldly presents,
because we should accept only
what the Master has given".
5. Then the Khvājā himself came to see Svāmījī,
with joined hands and bowing his head.
He said: "You are blessed, Dādū,
you are a pleasure to the Creator".
6. The greedy ascetic begged Dādū,
the joy-giver, to forgive him,
and the Khvājā came before Svāmījī, saying:
"You have experienced the indestructible King.
7. You and I are as different as the sun and a glow-worm.
You are like the sun, Svāmījī,
I am a glow-worm,
full of desires and illusions."

(28) In Mss. BEF we read: 'He introduced them into the state of no-fear'.

(29) Lit.: 'From the *Khvājā*', i.e. the tomb (*dargāh*) of the great fakir Khvaja-Mu'inu'd-Din Chishti the Sufi saint who died in Ajmer in 1234. In 1562 Akbar started his pilgrimage to this tomb. The Khvaja referred to in verses 13.5.5ff. must be a successor. Incidentally, "A story about the Kwaja during Akbar's period at Ajmer involved a dervish who visited him, and asked him what was expected of a true ascetic". See Rizvi:1978, p.123.

8. Svāmiji replied: "The Lord has shown you his mercy ,
placing all beings before you.
I know only Gosvāmi and I want no other.
Hari is in you and in me.
9. Besides the Master I want nothing else;
all other worship is useless.
Why do (Muslim) Sants strive after powers[30]?
Hari gives and to Him goes all praise.
10. Worship the Master only,
you should not be divided.
Rām stays far away from whatever
little worldly happiness you look for.
11. With great difficulty you earn the praise of the world:
this is the honour of (Muslim) Sants.
The eight perfections and the nine treasures
are the slaves of Hari: Sants keep away from them".

6. His worthy disciple Rajab
was full of wisdom, virtue and courage.
Having the temperament of an ascetic right from birth,
he gave up the world totally after meeting Svāmiji.
7. Rajab decided to organize a great festival
and invited Svāmiji.
He tried different ways to convince Svāmiji to come,
saying that the Indweller would shower His grace on them.
8. He urged him repeatedly,
till Svāmiji gave the order for the journey and
got on his way after a week.
He blessed the Sants he met on the way.
9. The first stop was Alhanyāvās
and everybody worshipped the Indweller:
Bohith, Khem Dās, Ṭikā,
Khetā, Tohā and Gobinda[31], all outstanding persons.
10. In Kārū[32] lived an ascetic called Ghaḍasī,
a man with the temper of a real ascetic.
His family held a great festival,
spending all they possessed.
11. Then they arrived in Kevalpur, where
all Sants gathered when they heard his name.
A great festival of devotion, with religious celebrations,
was organized for four days, to the great joy of Rajab.
12. Rāghav, Gobinda and Narāin were Rajab's disciples,
experienced in devotion.
Ṭhākur Dās invited him to Nīlyā,
making all the arrangements for his stay.
13. Govinda Dās also came there
and seeing Dādū his hope was fulfilled.
A great festival of devotion was held
and Svāmiji gave joy to all.
14. Then Svāmiji went to Pādū,
at the invitation of the devotee Ṭākū.
Kanhai of Keśav came there
and had the occasion to see Svāmiji.

(30) Lit.: Perfections *(siddhi)*.

(31) In Mss. BEF we read: Bohith, Rām Dās, Tikā (not Ṭikā), Govinda, Khetā, Kharathar.
See below vv.13.27 and 14.2.

(32) In Mss. BEF: Kālū.

1. He gave water as *prasād* to Ālhaṇ[33],
who took it with love and devotion.
Light shone within and without
and Ālhan reached the highest dwelling.
2. A miracle was performed at Ālhan's place,
when a two year old she-buffalo was milked.
Amazed at this, the people accepted Ālhan's authority
and his house became a shrine.

15. Jasvant, Jagannāth and Cāran Darsā
asked Dādū questions about his doctrine.
When a question came about *avatārs*,
they asked Svāmiji to explain it to them.
16. Svāmiji said: "Whatever has a beginning
will also have an end.
The Almighty is devoid of duality.
Meditate on this in your mind:
17. '*Dādū:* Brahma is not created,
He is not bound to a body,
He is unmoving, complete and undivided,
He is nectar and does not go around dancing on this world.'
18. In Pālari was the house
of the good devotee Kānhar Dās.
Leaving all illusion he surrendered (to Dādū)
and found truth in his presence.
19. In Īdawā Dūjan Sādh[34] lived near a pond,
in the shelter of Hari.
The ascetic Dūjan, essence of virtue,
always took charge of the meals for his guru.
20. There were also Rūpā, Jitā, Lakhū and Bāi,
Rāimal and Hāmā, givers of joy
and the good fellow Bāgh from Narbad,
a great favourite of Svāmiji.
21. Svāmiji gave joy to all
and all the Sants sang his praise.
He stayed in the monastery for a few days
and then, at the Master's order, he went his way.
22. Being a fervent devotee,
Rāy Singh learnt that Svāmiji was coming.
In Tyaudh he organized a great festival,
full of devotion and of love for Hari.
23. The devotees of the Dhūṇḍhar region
begged Svāmiji to come.
Dādū said: "Those ascetic devotees come first,
who love the Highest Guru."
24. Svāmiji left some devotees in the monastery.
Those who travelled with him are now named in the narrative:
Bāre Gopal, Sindhū, Pīpā, Candā and Bālā,
they all stayed close to him.
25. Keśav, Bābā[35]
Bhagvān, Mādhav and Sant Dās, all reliable followers.
Mohan Dās Daftari[36]

(33) See Sv. N. Dās:1975, pp. 850ff.
(34) In Mss. BEF we read: Dūjan Dās.
(35) Bālā in Mss. BEF.
(36) The meaning of *bācā* is not clear.

writes about the greatness of Hari
who is above the guru.
26. Paramānanda, of Pipā's descendency, and Kisna Dās[37],
had their minds full of bliss.
There were also the weaver Moni,
Dayāl Bengāli, Sādhū, Devendra and Vanmāli,
27. Santa Damodar, Dayāl Dās
and Paramānanda, the faithful disciples,
the good fellow Catur Dās Mardaniy,
Jagannāth, Mohan and Tikā[38]
28. The speakers Tejānanda and Mādhav,
the protectors Vyās and Sukhānanda,
Bāi Ramā and the brave Catur,
the searchers Jagannāth and Paramānanda,
29. the devotees Catur, Bhagvān Dayālū,
Rām Dās and Gopāl, all came.
Their numbers increased everyday,
as the rivers swell during the monsoon.
30. They saw Svāmiji and singing the praise of Hari,
they achieved fulfilment.
I have named the close disciples of Svāmiji,
but there are innumerable others.
31. After the first part of their journey
they arrived in Sāmbhar and
ascetics flocked together from everywhere.

Singing the wondrous deeds of Dādū Dinadayāl,
Jangopāl finds devotion to the Lord of the world
and finds liberation.

chapter 14

1. In Sāmbhar there were Maheś Dās and Govinda,
the faithful followers of Hari
Lāl Dās, Damodar and Khem,
the attractive Nādā, Sundar[39] and Prem.

2. Dāmodar and Tikā[40], two spiritual brothers,
and Haridās were givers of joy to Sants.
Remarkable, religious celebrations, lasting for eight days,
were held in Sāmbhar, with appropriate service to Svāmiji.

3. Bakhnā invited Dādū to Narainā.
Many Sants came to see him and experienced deep happiness.
Bakhnā organized fine celebrations
and Svāmiji stayed for a couple of days.

4. He was also invited to Bharainā by Ūdhav,
who organized religious celebrations, pleasing Dādū.
He further went to Bacūn, at the request of Mohan Dās,
a faithful follower of Hari, full of devotion.

(37) Dūbariyā in Mss. BEF.
(38) Tikā (not Ṭikā) in Mss. BEF; see above, 13.9, and below 14.2.
(39) *Sundar* may also be translated as 'beautiful'.
(40) Tikā (not Ṭikā) in Mss. BEF; see above, 13.9, 27 and below 14.19.

5. Then Taulhā invited him to Pūnyānā
and organized appropriate celebrations.
With great submission he performed *ārti* to Svāmījī,
who gave him the gift of devotion.

6. Laghu Gopāl, Ṭīlā and Chītar
invited him to Raṭanpur.
A suitable festival was organized for four days,
by the worthy devotee Udhav.

7. Kanakvatī, queen of Rāṭhor
and daughter of Ratan[41]
sent the family-priest
and Cārans [to Dādū].

8. She also sent Ben, the *kāyastha*,
with a firm invitation.
In Amer, people were overjoyed
and everywhere people proclaimed the name of Rām.

9. The queen organized a fine festival
and she came to see Svāmījī.
She donated clothes, presents and sweets,
but Dādū distributed everything and ate nothing himself.

> 1. When Mohan Dās Daftarī came to Sirūnj
> he performed many acts of devotion and inspired devotion in others.
> Seeing the devotees bringing good food,
> he reflected on their devotion.
> 2. He knew that their desires would be fulfilled,
> if Svāmījī would accept that food.
> He arranged to send a meal to Amer,
> to the place where Svāmījī was staying.
> 3. Ṭīlā asked who had brought the food
> and Svāmījī named Mohan Dās as the donor.
> Svāmījī ate a little during meditation
> and immediately he returned the meal to Sirūnj.

10. There was also Lāl Dās Mālī,
whose devotion and behaviour were outstanding.
Dhārū, Rūpā, Paramānanda and Rām Dās too
experienced divine bliss.

11. Without prior notice Svāmījī arrived in Karānjalī,
accompanied by the servants of the queen.
He gave them so much that
it was like experiencing liberation in life.

12. There was the joy-giving Rām Dās and Rānībāī,
the zealous follower of the guru.
Bīram, who had given up all sexual relationships,
came to touch Svāmījī's feet.

13. Experiencing Hari's love when meeting his guru,
Bīram invited everybody to Sāngāner.
With him went Haridās who hailed from Chātsū,
Udhav Dās and the devoted Nārāyaṇ.

(41) The second half of 7a is not clear. In the Sukh Dayāl Dādū edition (14.7) we read *dhori* for *ṭauri*, rendered as 'immersed in meditation' (*dhyān*).

14. Kārū, Kūmbhā and Narāin, all were disciples
experienced in devotion.
They organized a fine festival of seven days,
while camping in Kānautā.

15. There was also Narāin, the good grandson [of Dādū],
dedicated to the Lord of the world in thought, word and deed,
along with the disciples and companions of Jan Gopāl
and with Cain, another good grandson of Dādū.

16. Cain was overjoyed and
spent great sums in organizing a festival.
There were also Rām Dās, Mohan and Udhav,
Deī Dās, Lakhanā and Sūdhav.

17. Then Svāmījī made his entry
and fulfilled all the works of the Sants.
Religious celebrations were organized for three days,
by Kānhādās and his sister.

18. Nizām and Nāgar lived in a lonely hut,
where Svāmījī came to visit.
They performed the *ārti* to Svāmījī
and put the dust of his feet on their foreheads.

1. "We have given up the governorship of Ajmer[42]
and have come to seek your shelter.
We got involved in the world for the sake of a living,
but only you can take away our misery."

2. When Nizām and Nāgar made this plea before him,
Svāmījī gave them the highest insight[43], saying:
"Keep this pot upside down,
it will give food whenever you want."

19. A fourth celebration was organized
by Jan Gopāl and Jamunābāī, with Sūrharī, Tīkā[44],
Damodar and his brother Bālāhari,
all virtuous persons.

20. There were also Pīpā, Ṭhākur, Prayāg
and the ascetic Dayāl Dās;
Carandās, of the Rānkā clan,
and Gansī, firm of mind and a disciple of Svāmījī.

21. In the village Tahṭarā lived
the disciples Rānā, Gāṅgā, Sāngā and Bhagvān,
Rām Dās, Udhav and Keśav.
Then Dādū entered Dyausā.

22. There lived the worthy devotee Khem Dās
and his brother Mādhav with a mature mind,
and all the young disciples, the devotee Chājū
and Mathurābāī who did works of Hari.

(42) In *Dādū Caritāmrit*, Svāmī Nārāyaṇ Dās does not give this passage in the context of Jan Gopāl's story (II, p. 910ff.), but on I p. 565f.

(43) Lit.: "he gave them the capital", which is bigger when compared to Ajmer. The meaning is not certain.

(44) Tīkā (not Ṭīkā) only in Ms. G; see above v. 14.2 (etc.).

23. Also the outstanding Bohurā Narāin,
very generous and brave of heart.
Bhagvān Dās and Mādhav and Panda,
who hoisted the flag of devotion.

24. Svāmiji came to the house of Jagjivan,
who was really immersed in the Indweller.
While celebrations and a great festival were organized,
he stayed in Dūngar for a whole day.

25. There was the ascetic and musician Haridās,
who sang about Hari's qualities with an enlightened mind.
Also the ascetic Bhagvān Dās who gave up the world as *māyā*,
inspired by the company of Sants.

26. Then Svāmiji went to Kalyānpāṭan,
giving joy to Lakhā and Narhari.
With great devotion they performed *ārti*
and organized fine celebrations for two days.

27. All kinds of clothes were given as presents,
as had also been done by Khivā and Narāin[45].
There were also Syāmdās and Harikhābāi,
Hemi Banmāli and Tulsi, all joy-givers.

28. In Āndhi lived the worthy Dāmodar[46],
who had increased his love through earnest devotion.
He organized religious celebrations and a great festival,
giving joy to all the Sants.

29. The brothers Parbat, Bohith, Pūran
and Garib Dās organized celebrations,
along with the brother-in-law Khem Dās, with Keśav and Devrāj:
religious instructions were given to all.

30. There were also Caturā Viṣṇu Dās, Dhyān
and Balia, all experts in service.
Giving joy to all Svāmiji left
and went to see the devotees in Thoharāi[47].

31. Sūrahari met Svāmiji
when he came to Rāmhari[48].
There lived the brothers Caturbhuj and Rām Dās
and the devotee Khem Dās, all joygivers.

32. They organized a fine festival of devotion
and religious celebrations, praising Svāmiji.
Leaving instructions Svāmiji went on his way
and left for Ratanpur.

33. There Mādhav and Rām Dās were full of joy
and Svāmiji went further.
He took three days on his way to Sāmbhar,
where again celebrations were organized.

1. An ascetic there had evil thoughts

(45) Damodar in Mss. BEF.
(46) The first half of verse 14.28a is missing in Mss. CG.
(47) Modern Tholai.
(48) Rāhauri in Mss. BEF.

and intended to give Dādū a beating.
Svāmījī performed an amazing miracle
and appeared in the form of his opponent.
2. When the ascetic was beaten by his own disciple,
Dādū asked him why he did that.
The disciple replied: "Your glory is intolerable,
therefore my master has been punished."
3. After that the ascetic became frightened
and along with his disciple bowed down at Dādū's feet:
"Svāmījī, we are now your disciples.
Help us before we get drowned."
4. Dādū says: "If you want to beat someone,
you will be beaten yourself.
If you help someone reach liberation,
you will find liberation yourself"[49].

34. After that, the kind-hearted Dādū,
giver of joy, settled in Kalyānpur.
Dādū Dīndayāl gave joy to everyone.
His (grace) never runs dry, like rains during the rainy season.

chapter 15

1. Caturbhuj, the son of a noble man
came to see guru Dādū.
So now I'll will speak of Dādū's fame spreading to the East
and of the devotees who became associated with him.

2. I mention Jaimal of Baurī and Kisna Dās
who was always in (Dādū's) company.
Also Prahlād, the disciple of Syām Dās and
Pīpā who follows the rules laid down by the guru.

3. Kalyān Dās, Yādav, Tegvāru,
men of true character and reliable;
Rāmdas, Dāmodar the elder,
Dūdā, Hari and Bīram, all taking shelter with Hari.

4. There were also Lak simi Dās, Mādhav, Keśav
and Dharam Dās, listening to the guru's sermons.
A big crowd of Svāmījī's devotees gathered
and local celebrations were going on in Morḍā.

5. When Svāmījī arrived
he was praised in various ways.
People were happy to see him
and experienced bliss and joy.

6. *Ārtī* was performed, full of love
and all were in ecstasy.
Men and women were dancing and singing and
increased their love for the Supreme Lord.

1. Amazingly, all of a sudden it started to rain *keśar* flowers
and all the animals joined in the ecstasy.
The cows and oxen, as well as travelling merchants

(49) *Dādūvāṇī*, Caturvedi ed., v. 13.23

found liberation in this life.
2. All along this journey people in ecstasy sang praise.
Hearing Svāmiji's instructions
everyone found liberation,
merchants and oxen alike.

7. Having made them happy Svāmiji returned (to Kalyānpur),
and stayed there for one year.
In 1602 AD
the Master gave him a sign.

8. In 1603 he would leave this world,
for this is what the Master had decreed.

1. 'Dādū: I am happy with what pleases you
and accept whatever you say.
My heart rejoices in your truth,
day and night'[50].

9. Svāmiji understood he must die
and he reflected on what was coming[51].
He searched his mind for a place,
a pleasant village near a lake.

1. When Svāmiji had expressed his desire,
Hari gave an order to Narāin Dās
to take Svāmiji to Narāinā.
He thus came from the South.

10. Narāin Dās was the eldest son of the chieftain Jagmāi. Although he lived in the South
he had made a plan
at the request of his brother Durjansāl.

11. As Narāin Dās reached Narāinā,
Svāmiji also arrived there,
for his brother Amarā had been sent
to fetch Svāmiji.

12. The King was satisfied and ignored the Brahmans:
"We are fortunate that we have found such a treasure.
Anyone slandering him
will have to face Rām's mercy."

13. When Narāin Dās met Svāmiji,
it was as if the Indweller had appeared.
Holy instructions, singing and discussions were organized:
even a small participation fulfilled all purposes.

14. A place can be looked at from outside and from inside:
a wise person searches in the right place.

1. When Svāmiji came to Tripoliyā,
the snake-god Śeṣ appeared to him.
Śeṣ then made a sign
and Svāmiji made his seat there.

(50) *Dādūvāṇi*, Caturvedi ed., v.19.44.
(51) The meaning of *āgam* is not clear: it can mean 'revealed Shāstra, revelation' or 'what is coming' (*āgāmi*?).

A monastery was built on the bank of a small lake,
with a garden at the back, adjacent to the waters.

2. Dat, Gorakh, Prahlād, Nāmdev, Kabir
and the 84 Siddhas came to visit him.
They held religious discussions all night
and at dawn they disappeared.
3. Tilā asked Svāmiji:
"Who were you talking to all night?
They came and went, but we didn't see anyone,
even though the discussion lasted long into the night."
4. Svāmiji told the Sants: "Holy persons
appearing like Brahma have come.
The light of Brahma shone forth from them
and they made all darkness disappear."
5. 'When you meet a Santa you meet Hari,
they are the source of all happiness and bliss.
Dādū: The company of Sants
is full of the grace of Rām.'

15. Sants came from everywhere,
both householders and ascetics.
They performed menial service,
out of devotion for Hari and love for the guru.

16. After one month he came to the house
which was built at the instruction of Hari.
Ṭilā, Keśav, Govind Dās, Gopāl and Narhari
are the faithful devotees of Hari.

17. Another such house was very much needed
but Svāmiji insisted on staying there.
He gave instruction to all Sants
and performed a wonderful deed:

18. His body went into a state of concentration
and broke the shackles of illusion of all who were present.

1. As the moment of his death drew near,
he made his disciples firm in the devotion to the Name.
2. When Garib Dās knew that Svāmiji was going to die
he asked the following question:
"You have preached the path of the Unknowable
and removed the limitations of both Hindus and Muslims.
3. Hindus go to Benares and worship their gods,
while Muslims go to Mecca and honour the prophet.
You have abandoned the path of both.
How can we maintain this when you have gone?"
4. Dādūji said: "Brothers, keep my body
and for whatever you ask, you shall get a reply.
If you fear that my corpse will smell, remember
that it is not composed of the five elements.
5. If anybody still doubts,
let him rub his hand on my body and see.
My body is not real,
like a reflection in a mirror."
6. When they rubbed their hand over his body
they felt it was like a flame from a lamp.
They saw his body but could not grasp it with their hands
and they were astonished.
7. "Svāmiji, you are full of mercy

and the protector of all beings.
With such a miracle the whole world will come to see
and we shall be disturbed in our devotion."
8. He replied: "Whatever you ask, shall be answered
if you keep an oillamp burning here.
It will not require a wick or oil and
a mysterious light will always keep shining."
9. Garib Dās understood
that he should not pay attention to this miracle.
With miracles illusion arises and
this is an obstacle to reaching the Supreme Lord.
10. Seeing this spirit of detachment in Garib Dās,
Svāmiji said: "Rām is your protector.
This hut is the house of Hari.
Even when big crowds come, you will not be disturbed."
11. 'Dādū: I have put all my trust in Rām.
He will care for everything.
I see no one else,
for He takes care of things as He thinks fit'[52].
12. 'Take shelter in the Indestructible,
under the protection of the Ever-living.
Seek the protection of the True One
and you will never get hurt, says Dādū[53].'
13. If you stay firm in the *nirguṇ* devotion,
the Unknown will help you, and
there will be no room for the corruption of a personal deity[54].
Reflect and ponder on this."
14. Svāmiji spoke these true words
and Garib Dās kept them in his heart.
He clearly understood it and with the help of Svāmiji ,
he entered the state of fearlessness.
15. 'Dādū: Under the protection of the Master,
a person will come to no harm.
Even if the whole world is against you,
not a hair on your body will be hurt[55].
16. Then Garib Dās asked again:
"Svāmiji, you know what is coming.
Your ideas are in the minds of all the Sants,
but will there ever again be an accomplished Santa?"
17. Svāmiji made a revealed utterance:
"There will be an outstanding Santa after one hundred years."
In another couplet he said that
great disorder was to come and that,
18. If a person is firm in his devotion
to a personal deity, Rām will help him[56].
A drum was taken around the town
and all the people came to beat it.
The One Rām is the helper
of Prahlād, says Jangopāl.
19. Even at the end of time
our devotion will not disappear.
The *nirguṇ* devotion will never be destroyed
as long as Brahmā, Viṣṇu and Śiva are worshipped.
20. 'Dādū: Rām is Unmoving and
so devotion can not be described.

(52) *Dādūvāṇi*, Caturvedi ed., v.24.71
(53) *Dādūvāṇi*, Caturvedi ed.., v.25.65
(54) See below, v. 15.18.18.
(55) *Dādūvāṇi*, Caturvedi ed., v.24.75
(56) This line seems to contradict the condemnation of the devotion to a personal deity in verse 15.18.13.

Both are priceless, even if Śeṣ were
to sing of them with his thousand mouths'[57].
21. When there were no waters and no sun,
when the earth and the heavens did not exist,
when there was no moon and no sun,
even then Dādū Dās already existed.
22. For[58] the sake of liberation,
Dādū has appeared.
23. When there was no creation,
no shops or cloth,
even then Kabīr, the servant of Rām was there:
he has seen all that is good or evil.

Full of mercy he let the disciples come to him,
he took a bath and ate.

19. Then he went to sit in a lonely place
and the Blessed One gave him 3 commands.
One command was given first[59]
and at the second command his legs stopped.

20. At the third command Svāmījī
left his body to meet the Indweller.
It was 1603,
in the month of May[60].

21. On that Saturday, in the morning[61],
his close disciples realized that Dādū had died.
Pīpā informed Garīb Dās, and Maskīn Dās.
The elder Gopāl[62] Narāin

22. and the devotee Dūrgā,
men of firm devotion, were present.
Dayāl Dās and Rajab also came
to see Dādū at his death.

23. Ṭīlā was informed
and all the Sants gathered to meditate.
'Dāadū: My living body has been destroyed
in the fire of *virah*,

24. like a corpse in the grave,
long before I have reached my eternal dwelling'[63].

(57) *Dādūvāṇī*, Caturvedi ed., v.4.227

(58) The meaning of the expression *padamā padam ju caukaḍi* is not clear.

(59) The meaning of the line is not clear. The reading in the Sukh Dayāl Dādū edition is slightly different, with the following translation in Monika Thiel-Horstmann:1983b, p.115:

"As his first command he uttered: "Come",
As his second order the same *command*
was conveyed once again".

Strangely, this verse 19 has 3 lines in Mss. CG: after the first line of verse 18 we find 23 additional verses in Mss. BEF. Again, verse 25 has 3 lines in Mss. CG, thus matching again the numbering in Mss. CG and Mss. BEF.

(60) Lit: 'on the eighthday of the dark half of *jye sṭha*'. For an exact calculation of this date (12 or 22 May 1604), see M. Thiel-Horstmann:1983, p. 120-121.

(61) Lit.: 'when one fourth of the day had passed'.

(62) For the "three Gopāl's" (Bare Gopāl, Jan Gopāl and Laghu Gopāl), see *Ibidem*, p.121.

(63) *Dādūvāṇī*, Caturvedi ed., v.3.94 and v.23.52.

Everybody remained composed,
not venturing in or out[64].

25. Then they decided to take Svāmiji
to the holy hill in Bharainā.
A sedan chair had been brought two days earlier.
The corpse was anointed with saffron and sandal-paste.

26. It was taken to the hill[65],
as Svāmiji had ordered:
'The Creator will take care of everything,
you need not worry.'

27. On the hill there was a peak
where the chair of Rām was put down.
The fortunate devotees dressed
in shawls and long robes.

28. Special perfume, sandal-paste and *abir*[66] were applied
and all the devotees and Sants were calm.
They went down the hill singing hymns,
and hearing the news (of Dādū's death), all Sants were sad.

29. They all started to lament,
saying that no such holy man would ever appear on earth again.
Like a house without an oil-lamp, a night
without a moon and a child without a mother,

30. like a fish floundering out of water,
a goose without a lake and a calf without a cow,
so were the Sants grieving,
just as when Kabir, in this Kali age, left to go to Hari.

31. People came to see but those
who arrived first found only his clothes[67].
Others too came to search
but found no sign.

1. A miracle had occurred,
the chair had become invisible.
All the devotees and Sants gathered
and witnessed this wonderful event.
2. 'The body of Dādū and of Kabir
has disappeared like camphor.
Rajab: we have seen how miraculously a *saguṇ* body
is taken up in the light of the *nirguṇ* God.'
3. How could a jackal devour it or a fire consume it,
how could someone have buried the corpse?
Dādū met the Merciful One,
as salt disappears in water.
4. 'Dādū: when the heart needs the Merciful One,
there is no longer a distinction between the two.
The servant of Hari meets Hari

(64) We may translate this ambiguous line also as: 'nobody understood the external and the internal'.

(65) For a fine description of this site, see M. Thiel-Horstmann:1983, pp. 121-122.

(66) *Abir* is the red powder thrown on the occasion of Holi.

(67) We read 'sedan chair' in Mss. BEF. See further the interpolations in Mss. BEF (15.31.1 ff.).

as ice melts in water[68].'
5. 'Dādū: few can meet God by making their body subtle.
Many, however, can take their soul to God[69].'
6. Like camphor, the Santa looses his form, weight, shadow and smell.
Changing his stained body[70],
he is immersed in the Unstained.
Very few can understand this mystery.
7. In this Kali age Dādū was a great Santa,
taking up his body and flying away.
Forgetful humans do not understand
the mystery of Dādū becoming the Unstained God.

32. The Creator gave him the honour He gave to Kabīr.
What we had heard with our ears we have now seen.
Brahmā, Viṣṇu and Maheśvar, the holy men and the Siddhas,
all came forward (to welcome Dādū).

33. The Gandharvas came and praised (Dādū),
like children seeing their father.
Śiva invited him to Kailāś,
to stay with him in the abode of happiness.

34. Brahmā spoke to him about Brahmalok,
where death does not come till the end of time.
Viṣṇu invited him to Vaikuṇṭha
to drink nectar and to find complete happiness.

35. The Siddhas called him to Siddhalok,
where no desire for wealth or perfection would attract him.
The servant of (Hari) feels no temptations,
in him there is no attachment to the subtle or the gross.

36. With the Sants he sings the praises of (Hari),
immersed in the Supreme Brahma he has found the truth.
Gopāl says: nobody knows the state of Dādū Dīnadayāl,
his body and soul are immersed in light, as water is in water.

chapter 16

1. Garīb Dās organized everything so well,
it is beyond description.
After Svāmījī's death he took great care
to maintain everything as it had been.

2. With great determination he sent letters to many people.
Both the ascetic and the faithful wife
show their greatness through courage:
through their actions they destroy attachments.

3. The bamboo shoot grows to be bamboo
and in a forest of sandaltrees everything smells like sandalwood.
From a lioness a lion is born
and an ascetic walks on the path of the Siddhas.

(68) *Dādūvāṇī*, Caturvedī ed., v.4.278.
(69) *Dādūvāṇī*, Caturvedī ed., v.4.185.
(70) For *añjan* turning into Nirañjan, see M. Thiel-Horstmann:1983b, p. 122.

4. Sants came from all around when they heard the news
as during the rainy season clouds gather in the sky.
Many tents were pitched
as if the Emperor were travelling.

5. They settled near the pond in great numbers,
in the village, in gardens, in houses and in the open fields.
The important Sants were settled first;
the others were told to come afterwards.

6. The disciples Sāṅgā, Jasā, Paharāj,
Bohith and Dev did the work of Hari.
Also present were Khem Dayāl Dās and Pipā,
Banmāl and the devotee Bisna.

7. Garib Dās collected all the provisions, with a pure mind
and total generosity, not considering the cost.
Rice, lentils, wheat, ghee, flour and sugar
were supplied in abundance.

8. Some took uncooked rice
while others had prepared meals.
The celebrations were organized in May
and lasted for a full month[71].

9. For the whole month the religious celebrations continued
and all Sants were given festive attire.
All supplies contributed to the celebrations
were donated by the homes.

10. Great quantities of *phirnī* were made,
because this had been a favourite sweet of Svāmiji.
There were the disciples Rām Dās,
Baghā, Narāin and Devī Dās,
all well accomplished in devotion to Hari.

11. Day and night the singing went on,
everybody was singing joyfully.
All Sants were given clothes,
thin cloth for (filtering) water and a loin-cloth.

12. Wrinkled leaves drop during March[72],
but in December everything looks green again.
Garib Dās provided everyone with clothes,
giving to all who had come from outside.

13. He had thick clothes distributed to everybody
and made no distinction between outsiders and followers.
Dried coconuts, dates, clover and sweets
were continuously given in abundance.

14. The Almighty was so pleased
that the food kept multiplying[73].
There were no stored provisions,
but Hari, the yielding Gem, provided all that was needed.

(71) Lit.: 'The celebrations were organized around the full moon of May, lasting from one new (i.e. dark) moon to the next new moon'.

(72) *Caitra* starts with the new moon of March. *Paus* starts with the new moon of December.

(73) Lit.: 'as things were distributed they kept increasing by one quarter.'

15. Hari does His own work and gives the credit
to His devotee, making firm his status.

15.1. Hari did what His name[74] implies,
allowing the glory of His deeds to be accorded to Garib Dās.

'The Self accomplishes everything himself, but gives the credit to others.
Glory goes to the devotee, He never names Himself[75]

16. The Sants anointed Garib Dās as the successor,
he was given the seat and place of the guru.
Garib Dās began to be considered as equal to Svāmiji,
with the support of the Sants.

17. Anyone who sings, hears or reflects (on my tale)
will become devoted to Rām in his heart.
Even the ignorant will acquire wisdom,
their minds will begin to meditate on the Supreme Brahma.

18. If a fool hears it, he will acquire knowledge,
if a pauper hears it, he will acquire wealth.
Whatever a man desires, in his heart or through words,
that will sureley come to pass.

19. If a Santa hears it he will be exceedingly joyful
and deep understanding will be given to him.
But if a wicked man hears it, he will be greatly pained
and in his heart he will turn to an incarnate God (*banavāri*).

20. The devotee, who sings of Hari with a firm mind,
He attains the final goals of both devotion and deliverance.
All devotees are in truth forms of (Rām) Himself,
for they love no one else.

21. Rām Himself is happy when the devotees are happy,
when they eat He is satisfied.
When a devotee is made to suffer, Hari Himself suffers,
He comes running after His devotees.

22. Though He is said to be omnipresent,
He can only be found in His devotees.
Milk exists in every pore of the cow, but it[76]
can only be found in the udder.

23. 'Dādū: Brahma is the cow (pervading) the three worlds;
the devotees (alone) can drink from its udder.
Nectar rains from the mouths of the Sants,
why should you look for it elsewhere[77]?'

24. If the seven oceans were made into an inkpot and
a hundred thousand Meru mountains were poured in as ink;
if all the trees in this world were made into pens
and Sarasvati herself were to write, she would not be able to complete this story.

(74) *Cintāmaṇi* or 'Fulfiller of desires'.
(75) *Dādūvāṇi*, Caturvedi ed., v.21.22 and v.35.6.
(76) *Nir* means 'water', 'beauty, splendour'.
(77) *Dādūvāṇi*, Caturvedi ed., v. 15.29

25. Even if the entire earth were made into paper,
(it would not suffice to write) the merits of Rām and His devotees.
What I have said is limited by my understanding.
Let no one be pleased or hurt.

26. Dādū spent twelve years as a child and
then he met his guru who appeared before him.
In 1573 he came to Sambhar
and in 1575 Garib Dās was born.

27. In 1585 he met Emperor Akbar
and in 1593 he went to Kalyānpur.
In 1602 he came to the town of Narainā
and in 1603 he became one with Rām.

28. I am the devotee Gopāl, an ascetic and a Baniyā.
My true guru is Dādū, the merciful one.
It was my great good fortune that I found shelter with him.
I sang the praises of that greatest of Sants.

29. I have sung of the great festival organized for Dādū.
I have firm faith in Garib Dās to whom I surrender myself.

Thus ends the *Janmalilā* of Dādū.

CHAPTER 3

Hindi Text

One

1 नमो निरंजन देव गुसांई गुर प्रसाद थैं सब सुधि पाई ।
सब संतनि कौं बंदन कीजै भगति प्रताप रांम-रस पीजै ।
2 सत त्रेता द्वापर कलि मांही तिन के संत अंत कहूं नांही ।
जे प्रसिध सुनें ते गाऊं और सबनि कौं माथौ नाऊं ।
3 स्यौ सनकादिक अरू सुषदेऊ ध्रू प्रहिलाद करी हरि सेऊं ।
नांम कबीर भये रैदासा पीपा सेन धना हरदासा ।
4 औरौं संत बुरी जिनि मांनौ गुर दादू कौ सुजस बषानौं ।
1 अदभुत बात कही नहीं जाई कैसै रसना कहूं बनाई ।
बेद कुरान पुरान न जांनै मनिष कहा मुष करै बषानै ।
रसना एक अल्प मति थोरी बरनी जाइ न लाष करोरी ।
5 संबत सोलह सै इकोतर संत एक उपज्यौ पहुमी पर ।
पछिम दिसा अहमदाबादू तिहि ठांई साध प्रगट्यौ दादू ।
1 निजानंद नित ब्रहम अपारा नित की आग्या सौं तन धारा ।
सब जीवनि की पूरी आसा भगति हेत हरि कीयौ बिलासा ।
2 सबदि बधांणा साह कौ नाथै दादू आया ।
दुनिया जीवी बापुरी सषि दरसण पाया ।
3 जैसैं नभि मैं बादर आवैं करि प्रमारथ तहां समावैं ।
यूं हरि आग्या सौं जन आये भगति करी हरि मांहि समाये ।
6 धुनिया कै घरि भयौ अनंदू मानु उग्यौ दुतिया चंदू ।
माता पिता षरे बडभागी जिनि के सुत हरि सौं ल्यौ लागी ।
1 इक सौदागर अहमदाबाद मंझारा येक पुत्र कौ फिरै बिचारा ।
गैबी संत मिल्यौ तिहि बारा करि बीनती इक बचन उचारा ।
2 सुणैं स्वामी इक अरज हमारी पुत्र बिनां दुष है मोहि भारी ।
तब उरनि संति इक ग्यरा उचारी जाऊ समंद पहि बडी संचारी ।
3 बडी सबेर सो समंद पहि जावै बालक अधर तिरतौ सो आवै ।
गोद मांहि तब ले घरि आयौ गैबी दूध माता कै पायौ ।
4 सिध सकित करि पलटी काया बाल का रूप है दरस दिषाया ।
इहि बिधि सांमीं तज्यौ संघासन मोहन मिवाडै देष्यौ आसन ।
5 अैसी बिधि लीना अवतारा अचिरज मांन्यौ सब संसारा ।
मात पिता कै भयौ आनंदा मानूं आज मिल्यौ गोब्यंदा ।
6 मुकंद भारथी कही जु गाता जैमल हमारौ नांहीं माता ।
महापुरष प्रगटै हैं आदू जैमल का गुर स्वामी दादू ।
7 अैसौ पुरष प्रगट्यौ सोई तीनि कोडि पारंगति होई
जब माता कह्यौ दरसन क्यूं पईये ज्यूं प्रपति है त्यूं ही कहिये ।

3 A 1 सिब D BEF
4 A 3-5 जु सबै मनाऊ BEF ;9 सुनाऊ BEF
5 A 2 सोला BEF
6 A 1 सब संतनि BEF ;7 प्रगट्यौ A

8 अब माता सुणि सति बचन हमारा अहमदाबादि लीयौ औतारा ।
फुनि सांभरि आवैरि सु आसी तब तूं भी उनको दरसन पासी ।
9 इतनूं बचन गुसांई भाष्यौ माता जैमलि हिरदै राष्यौ ।
राति दिवस यहु ध्यान बिचारै कदि स्वांमी आवैरि पधारै ।
7 तीजै पहर निकटि ही संझा षेलत हुते लरकनि मंझा ।
जब बीते ऐकादस बरसूं बाबा बूढै दीनौं दरसूं ।
8 परम पुरिष परमेसुर गांमी देई अभैपद अंतरजांमी ।
भौ संसार तिरै अरू तारै रिधि सिधि मुकति सदा दरबारै ।
9 मांग्यौ आनि पईसा ऐकूं सब काहूं कौ लेइ बमेकूं ।
दीनौं स्वांमी बार न लाई रीझे बाबा सब सुषदाई ।
10 बालक दसा जाहि मति ऐसी कौंन रती याकै सिरि बैसी ।
बिगसे बाबा निकटि बुलाये सकल सरीर हाथ तब लाये ।
11 सरस तंबोल दीयौ मुष मांहीं रांम देई मेटै कोनांहीं ।
1 येक बूंद पग ऊपरि आई चरनौ लागि मुकति है भाई ।
चारि षूंट मैं प्रगट भईया दादू दादू घटि घटि कहीया ।
श्रबसु दै माथै कर दीनौं बालक बुधि जांनि नहीं लीनौं ।
12 बरिष सात औरौं कृत कीनौं ता पीछैं हरि दरसंन दीनौं ।
पंथ चलत उपजाई ऐसी बाहरि दृष्टि सो भीतरि पैसी ।
1 जिहाज ब्यौहार पिता कै भाई स्वांमी हरि की भगति चलाई ।
पैसा बसत्र अंन भंडारा मिलै अतीत लुटावै सारा ।
2 तब घर कें जुदा करि दीया जब स्वांमी उनका दरब न लीया ।
तब करै तलाई षाय षुलावै पैंडा पैंड परि हरि गुन गावै ।
3 अब स्वामी कै मनि ऐसी आई जग ब्यौहार दीयौ छिटकाई ।
छाड्यौ देस तज्यौ घर बार सासैं सांस भजै करतार ।
13 देष्यौ ब्रह्म जोति प्रकासू आतमरांम हि भयौ निवासू ।
पीछै बोली आकासबांणीं धंनि धंनि दादू जगि जांणीं ।
14 तब थैं बिसरि गयौ संसारु निसदिन कीनौं ग्यान बिचारु ।
चींटी कुंजर समि करि देषै लोहा कंचन ऐक बसेषै ।
15 निंदया अस्तुति ऐक समांनां सब ही जीवनि मैं भगवांनां ।
परधंन परत्रिया थैं न्यारौ निसदिन कीजै पर उपगारौ ।
1 दरस काजि उमग्यौ संसारा ग्यांन कौ करै बिचारा ।
बरण आसरम की मिटी सगाई यौं हरिजन हरि मांहि समाई ।
16 रूई धुनैं अरू षाइ षुलावै सांचै कहु न चित डुलावै ।

7A 7 होते D BEF ;B 5-8 बूढै रूप दियौ हरि दरसू BEF
8A 5 दीयौ BEF
9A 2 आई CG
11A 3 दियौ D BEF
11B1 सरबस D BEF
12A 3-10 रहे घरि माई फिरि दरसन दीयौ निरंजनि राई BEF
12B9 बैसी BE
14A 8 कीयौ A कीजै D BEF ;B 2 कुंजर CG F
16A 1-2 सहज मैं आवै BEF

दीनौं लेइ न बाछै काऊ निज सेवक सेवा कौ भाऊ ।
17 दया धर्म जिहि बसै सरीरं मानहु औतरे दास कबीरं ।
रहनि कहनि करनी सब सारी दूवै पष रहत साध मति भारी ।
18 दादूदीनदयाल कौ जनम कहै सुनै कोई ।
जनगोपाल जगदीस की भगति अषंडित होई ।

Two

1 फुनि सांभरि कौं कीयौ पयांनौं बाढी प्रीति बिरह अधिकांनौं ।
पारब्रह्म सौं तारी लागी गुप्त जोति अंतरगति जागी ।
2 नष सष सुमिरण नांव कहावै आतम बिसरै अंगि समावै ।
झिलिमिलि नूर तेज नित देषै जीवन जनम सुफल करि लेषै ।
3 उपजी अनभै ग्यांन अनंता कहौ कबीर मिलैं भगवंता ।
मिले कबीर समाधिक जागै ब्रह्म गोष्ठि संसै सब भागै ।
4 पद सौं पद साषी सौं साषी रहति कहति सारीषी भाषी ।
तब अनभै कौ भयौ बिसासूं जब थैं मिले कबीरा दासूं ।
5 तुरकी राह षोदि सब गाडी अरू हींदुनि की करनी छाडी ।
षट दरसन सौं नांही संगा निसदिन रहै रांम कै रंगा ।
6 स्वांग भेष पष पंथ न मांनैं पूरनब्रह्म सति करि जांनैं ।
देवी देव न पूजा पाती तीरथ ब्रत न सेवा जाती ।
7 हींदू तुरकनि झगरौ कीनौं सब काहू कौं उतर दीनौं ।
काजी बांभन सब पचिहारे कहा करै जौ हरि रषवारे ।
1 जौ हम नहीं गुजारते तुम्हकौ क्या भाई ।
सार नहीं कहु बंदिगी कहु क्यूं फुरमाई ।
2 दादू कहै फूटी नाव समंद मै सब डूबण लागे ।
अपणां अपणां जीव ले सब कोई भागे ।
8 बांभन बनियां फिरि मत कीनौं पंचाइत कौं सोधौ दीनौं ।
कागद लिष्यौ दुहाई देहू हमारे जांन भलौ मतु ऐहू ।
9 जौ कौऊ दादू कै जैहै सैका पांच रूपईया दैहै ।
लिषि सिकदार डौंडी दई सांची अषिर फिरे बहुरि जब बांची ।
10 दादू कै जोई नही जैहै सैका पांच रूपईया दैहै ।
तब थैं सांभरि उपज्यौ भाऊ साध बडौ दरसन सब पांऊं ।
11 तब आयौ काजी अजमेरी हाथि कतेब राह क्यूं फेरी ।

17A 6 मनहु A BEF मानौं D ;B 4 अति CG

1B 5 गुपत A BEF
2A 9 लगावै A ;B 4 निज D BEF
3A 4 अपारा BEF ;5 - आयौ कबीर तुरत तिहि बारा BEF
3B 3-4 समाधि जगाई BEF ;6 - सौं अति रूचि बढाई BEF
4B 4 कियौ BEF
9A 1 जे D

मुसलमांन कलमां थैं होइ रामु कहैं काफर हैं सोइ ।
1 काफिर सो जो बोलै काफ दिल अपणी नहीं राषै साफ ।
सांई कूं पहिचांनै नांही कूंड कपट सबउ नही मांही ।
12 स्वांमी कह्यौ सुनौं हो काजी भूलौ कहा देषि यहु बाजी ।
मुसलमांन दीन की धरनी हींदू चलै आपनी करनी ।
13 कौंन पंथ परमेसुर भावै बूझै हमहि कि बेगि बतावै ।
कौंन धर्म जहां आतमघाता सब जग दीसै दोजगि जाता ।
14 काजी षिज्यौ कौंस की दीनीं स्वांमी धंनि बोडि मुषि लीनीं ।
दूजी घा मुष बोड़यौ आई अबकै करौ हमारी भाई ।
15 ऐकै कौंस लोक यहु सूझ्यौ दूजी देतौ तौ करता बूझ्यौ ।
कठिन सरीर आहि अंति मेरौ काजी हाथ दुषि है तेरौ ।
16 सुकच्यौ काजी घरि उठि जाई परमेसुर तब बांह.दुषाई ।
काजी कहै बुरी मैं कीनीं साहिब कै मुषि कौंसा दीनीं ।
17 मास तीनि पीरा दुष पायौ काजी मरत बहुत पछितायौ ।
जौ संतनि सौं करै बुराई सत्यानास प्रलै है जाई ।
18 दादूदीनदयाल की उपजनि सब सुष सार ।
जनगोपाल कहै सुनैं सोइ उतरै पार ।

Three

1 सांभरि मैं काजी अभिमांनी स्वांमीं सौं ज बैरता ठांनी ।
अबकै जाइ गाइ है आंऊं पीछै याहि सजा हूं लाऊं ।
2 गांडू षोदि गलै लौं देहा सिर परि करौं बांन कै बेहा ।
तुपक तीर नेजे संमसेरी सतपंथरी कटारी हेरी ।
3 यौं कतेब मै हैं फुरमाया मुसलमांन क्यूं कुफर चलाया ।
तब ही रहै दीन की बाता बेईमांन षलक है जाता ।
4 अंतरजांमीं बात बिचारी संत बैर बिन होइ न ष्वारी ।
मंन सै सात रुई घर मांहीं परजरि उठी अगनि ढिग नांहीं ।
5 लागी लाइ कुटंब सब जरियौ ता पीछै काजी अंति डरियौ ।
तब थैं कहू बैर नहीं कीनौं ताहू कौं स्वांमी सुष दीनौं ।
6 नगर निकासि गये फुनि स्वांमीं नीकै सुमिरै अंतरजांमीं ।
मातौ हाथी सनमुष आयौ भाज्यौ लोक दसौं दिसि धायौ ।

11B 1- कलमै बिना भिस्त नहीं BEF
13A not AG
14A 3 षौंस CG
15A 2 षौंस CG ;7 देतां A देहु C दे D
16A 1 संकुच्यौ CG
17B 1 जो AD BEF

1A 4 अधिकारी A ;8 बैरतउ C बैरताउ G
2A 4 लुं CG ;9 बांनन BEF
5A 6-8 जा दिन तैं BEF

7 स्वामी कहु संक नहीं कीनी अंतरजांमीं लीनौं चीनीं ।
गज आवै माया मद छाक्यौ हम तौ सदा रांम रस चाष्यौ ।
8 तब हाथी ठाढौ है रहियौ दरसंन देषि सबै सुष लहियौ ।
चरन छुया अरू माथौ नायौ स्वांमी हाथ सीस तब लायौ ।
9 फुनि तसकर आयौ घर मांही ढूढै तौ संचित कछू नांही
पायौ सूत लैंन जब लाग्यौ आहट भयौ कुटंब सब जाग्यौ ।
10 सासू त्रिया कहैं जु दोई कौंन हाल घर भीतरि होई ।
पुरिष रूप दीसै घर मांही तसकर हू सौं बोलै नांही ।
11 स्वांमी कह्यौ बेगि जा भाई जौलौं काहू सुधि न पाई ।
जौ जागिहै पाहरू कोई तोहि मरण हंमकौं दुष होई ।
1 तब तसकर मन मैं पछिताया महापुरष मेरा जीव बचाया ।
लेय प्रसाद स्वामी पैं आया चोरी छोडि सिष्य कहाया ।
12 दिवालै स्वांमी पद गावै काजी तुरकनि कौं नही भावै ।
मिलि दस बीस पकरि लै आये दसौं दिसा थैं मारन धाये ।
13 तन थैं सुरति निरंतरि राषी तबही तुचा मृतक करि नाषी ।
मंन भावै ते ताल कर लीनां दोऊ हाथ काष मैं दीनां ।
14 वै पापी पतित क्रोध अरू कांमीं स्वांमी देषैं अंतरजांमीं ।
कोउ पूजै कोउ मारै साधु सब घटि रांम बिचारै ।
15 बहुर्‍यौं षोजा पै लैं जांही दुष पायै पापी पछितांही ।
फूनि बिलदि षोजा हठ कीनौं स्वांमी पकरि भाषसी दीनौं ।
16 कौंण करामाति छाडी राहा आंपण बिगडि षलक कौं बाहा ।
परमेसुर तब प्रीति बिचारी जैसैं बालक दूष दूषहं महंतारी ।
17 बाहरि भीतरि दरस दिषायौ तब षोजा कौ तिमर नसायौ ।
बकसौ यहु अपराध हंमारौ हंम क्या जांनैं मरम तुम्हारौ ।
18 स्वांमीं कह्यौ दोस नही तुम्हकौं करता करै सु भावै हंमकौं ।
सब ही नगरि सुनीं यहु बाता आनि महोछै ठाटे साता ।
19 स्वांमीं पौढि रहे घर मांही भगति महोछै जांनैं नांही ।
करनहार ऐसी कछू कीनीं काहू पै गति जाइ न चीन्हीं ।
20 जोई भगत बुलांवन आवै स्वांमी रूप तहां उठि धावै ।
भगति महोछै अंति रस राष्यौ बाढी प्रीति प्रेम रस चाष्यौ ।
21 सब कौ कहै कथा यहू आदू सात महोछै स्वांमीं दादू ।
स्वांमीं पूछै बात न मांनैं अबिगति की गति अवगति जांनैं ।
22 दह दिसि महिमां मांनि बडाई दरसंन कारनि दुनियां धाई ।

7A 7-8 लीन्हीं AD BEF
9B 1-2 पोथी पाना BEF ;8 संत BEF
10A सेवग संत कहैं सुषदाई कौंन है घर भीतरि भाई BEF
11B 1 जे BEF
12A 5 हीदू A
13B 6 लीनें A BEF लीने D ;7 दौऊ CG ;11 दीनें A BEF दीने D
15A 1 बहुरि D BEF ;B 2 बलिंदषान BEF
16B 5 ज्यौं BEF

1 दोइ सिध स्वांमी पै आया घोडे देषि रू मुष मुलकाया ।
तब स्वामी कह्यौ कहा दिल दीया नीलै कान सु आगै कीया ।
2 तब स्वामी कह्यौ कछु बस्त न पाइ षाली सिधि मैं क्या है भाइ ।
दून्यूं सिध यूं बोल्या जाई पूरै गुर थैं बस्त सु पाई ।
3 दादू देषे का अचिरज नहीं अणदेषे का होइ ।
देषे ऊपरि दिल नहीं अणदेषे कौ रोइ ।
सबही भगत लोग चलि आयौ छीतर गैबी दरसंन पायौ ।
23 तब बांनें की बात चलाई स्वांमी दादू कौं नही भाई ।
1 दादू सतगुरि माला मन दीया पवन सुरति सौं पोइ ।
बिन हाथौं निसदिन जपै प्रम जाप यूं होइ ।
कहा करौं ऐ ठां तुरकांनौं हिंदवांनैं पहराऊं बांनौं ।
24 तब स्वांमी आंबैरि बिचारी सुमिरण कौं ठाहर अंति भारी ।
दादूदीनदयाल कौ परचौ परंम प्रसिधि ।
जनगोपाल कहै सुनैं सो जांनैं सब बिधि ।

Four

1 आंबानेरी स्वांमीं आये राजा परजा कै मंनि भाये ।
निसदिन भीर होइ दरबारा कथा कीरतन ग्यांन बिचारा ।
2 पूरब पछिम उतर दषिन आवैं साध संत बिचछन ।
बहु बिधि लोक दरसंन कौं आवैं भगति भाव करि भेंट चढावैं ।
3 स्वांमी ऐक हाथ नहीं छींवैं छाजंन भोजंन सहज सु कीवैं ।
1 राति दिवस भीर अति होई अंतर परै भजन मैं सोई ।
तब रुई धूनन कौ किसब जु लीनूं भीर मिटन कौं उदिम कीनौं ।
2 हमरै दरसि आवौ मति कोई किसब हमारा देषौ सोई ।
ज्यूं ज्यूं स्वामी आप छिपावै त्यूं त्यूं दुनिया अधिकी आवै ।
3 बंदा लघुता अपनी करई पट कै परदै दीप न दुरई ।
स्वामी अपनी मांनि मिटावै त्यूं त्यूं साहिब अधिकी लावै ।
4 गुन डोरी नीची षसत ग्यान दीप आकास ।
रजब उलटे पेच कौं समझै समझादास ।
पहलै कछू रुई क्रित कीनौं फुंनि माधूकर भोजंन लीनौं ।
4 लौंग छवारी गिरी मिठांई दीजै बांटि गांठि नहीं भाई ।
पान फूल आवैं त्यूं जांहीं मातौ रहै रांम रस मांहीं ।
5 राजा परजा दरसंन पावै तापैं रुइ कौं न बिहनावै ।
1 दरसन कौं सब अरज बषांनैं धुनि मैं गरक जगत सब जांनैं ।
प्रा सबद आयौ आकासा रुई धुनैं मति है जग नासा ।
2 मरम तुम्हारौ जाणैं नांहीं न्यंदा करि कै नरकि परांहीं ।

22B 1-5 रांम गटा अर जंगी आयौ CG
23A 8-9 कौं है CG ;B 3 इहि D BEF

2A 8 बिचिषिन A बिचक्षण D बिचछिन BEF ;B 4 दरस AD BEF
3B 1-2 दिन दूवै चारि BEF
4A 2 छुहारा AD BEF

न्यंदग कीया यहु फल होई दोजगि परै राषै नहीं कोई ।
3 तब तैं स्वामी रूई न पीनी अषंड सुरति ब्रह्म मैं दीनी ।
ज्यूं कबीर गनिका संग्य लीनी तै सैं स्वामी रूई पीनी ।
4 ज्यौं ज्यूं स्वामी आप छिपाया त्यूं हरि प्रगट कीया सवाया ।
पींजंन रहै प्यलंग सिरहांनैं धूनियां जाति कमीन बषानै ।
6 छाडी नहीं सैंन हरि छूटी बहूं बासनां जगत मैं फूटी ।
1 ज्यूं कबीर नामदे धू प्रहलादू त्यूं ही प्रगटे स्वामी दादू ।
जब स्वामी आंबैरि पधार्‌यौ तब जैमलि वहु सुष न संभार्‌यौ ।
2 वह कह्‌य गुसांई सुषन जु माता अब आये स्वांमी सब सुष दाता ।
ज्यूं कह्‌य गुसांई त्यूं ही जु आया तब जैमलि माता दरसन पाया ।
3 अब माता जाइ स्वामी स्यूं आषी मुकंद भारथी जैसै भाषी ।
अैसै संति लीया औतारा तीनि कोडि का होइ उधारा ।
4 धनि गुसांई जिनि नाव बताया तब तुम्हारा दरसन पाया ।
उनि साधि कह्‌यौ अपनै उन्माना तीनि कोडि का कहा बषाना ।
5 जब लग जिमी अकास रहाई तब लग आत्म उधरै माई ।
न्यिरगुण भगति की बाधी पाज अनंत कोटि के सीझैं काज ।
6 माथै हाथ स्वांमी तब दीया जैमल कूं जब सेवग कीया ।
कृपा करि मस्तकि दीया हाथ भये बदेह जैमल अरू मात ।
7 जग ब्यौहार की छाडी रीति हरि सुमरण सौं लागी प्रीति ।
जो ठग दादू जाइ कहावै ताहूं की हरि पूजा लावै ।
8 महापुरष कै नाई बिकाया ठग बाजी तजि सरनै आया ।
स्वामी कौ सिष माधौदासा सहर सीकरी लीयौ निवासा ।
9 सहजि देहुरै बैठै जाई मुरति दिसा पीठि करि भाई ।
साषति लोगनि आंनि उठायौ तूं हूं कहा नामदे आयौ ।
10 नामदे कहा कीयौ भाई पै पायौ रू गऊ जिवाई ।
अबहू सम्रथ करै सु होई पीवै दिवाल देषै सब कोई ।
11 राम नाम निज हिरदै धरई ज्यूं जन कहै त्यूं ही हरि करई ।
तुरसी बांभण न्यंदक भाई ताकौ माधौदास जमाई ।
12 सो मन मैं दाधौ दुष पाई पातसाहं स्यूं जाइ सु नाई ।
राष्या रोकि जु माधौ भाई स्यंघ कैं प्यंजरै दीया ज राई ।
13 तब माधौदेव लगाई तारी डरप्या स्यंघ सु उलटा भारी ।
फजर हूवा तैं षबरि मंगाई सुकच्यौ स्यंघ ज्यूं डरै निलाई ।
14 अकबरि देष्यौ भये प्रभाति यहु फकर अलह की जाति ।
अकबरि कह्‌या फक्र यहु नीका तब तुरसी का मुष हूवा फीका ।
15 तुरसी कह्‌यौ ताहि छिटकावो ताके पीरहि बेगि बुलावो ।
7 साहि अकबर सुंनी सु बाता परवानैं पंठवै दिन राता ।
स्वांमीं जाइ न सौं सुष पावैं संमझि संमझि मन मैं पछितावैं ।
8 तब राजा भगवंतदास सुनाई तुम्हारे स्वांमीं सब सुषदाई ।

5B not BEF
6:5B 1 न्यरगुण E निरगुण F
7B 4 सो AD BEF

बहु बिधि सुनौं नांव प्रकासूं मांनूं लीयौ कबीर निवासूं ।
9 बोलै कहु न आवै जांहीं हमकूं दरसन देई क नांहीं ।
तब राजा उठि बिनंती कीनीं पातिसाह कौं धीरज दीनीं ।
10 फूंनि राजा डेरै पछितांनौं परमेसुर हौं कियौ अयांनौं ।
सुष दुष स्वांमीं कबहू न आवै पतिसाह तब षरौ रिसावै ।
11 दुचितौ राजा पांन न षाई तब सूजा षीची सुधि पाई ।
आहिसु देह बेगि लै आंऊं ऐहै मिसि हौं दरसंन पाऊं ।
12 पाती दई बार नहि लाई बहल कही अरु मुहर बधाई ।
ल्यावहु बेगि बार नही लागै पातिसाह हमपैं यौं मांगै ।
13 तब सूजा आंबेरि पधार्‌यौ दरसंन देष र जंनमु सुधार्‌यौ ।
पाती दई रू संदेस सुनायौ स्वांमी तुम्हीं लैनहूं आयौ ।
14 कौंन काज काहे कूं भाई हंमारै काज न रांनां राई ।
पातिसाह राजा हठ कीनौं दरस देषि हम लाहौ लीनौं ।
15 चलण कहौ तौ हूं घरि जांऊं नांतर पांनी अंन न षांऊं ।
स्वांमी कह्यौ जाह घर भाई करता करै सु है है आई ।
16 स्वांमी बात रांम परि राषी ध्यांन सैंन चलिबे की भाषी ।
तब संतनि कौं कह्यौ बिचारू मंनसा बाचा हरि रषवारू ।
17 जौ न चलैंहि करिहै बरियाई पीछै रहूं तौ लोग हसाई ।
तब चलिबे कौ उदिम कीनौं सब संतनि कौं आइसु दीनौं ।
18 संतदास दूवारै तब राषे तेई बचन दमोदर भाषे ।
गरीबदास की सेवा कीज्यौ दूवारिकादास बचन सुनि लीज्यौ ।
19 चांदा टीला लीने साथा जगजीवन स्यूं कही जु गाथा ।
स्यांमदास लाहोरी भाषे जंन जगदीसदास संगि राषे ।
20 संग गुनदास बादरा बैंसी धरमदास गुर संग मति गैंसी ।
सात सिष ले स्वांमी चले जंनगोपाल सीकरी मिले ।
1 सब संतां मिलि अरज बिचारी बादिसांहां सौं मिलणा भारी ।
नाम कबीर प्रहलाद की साषी तब स्वामी अपणी निहचै आषी ।
2 दादू मडा न जीवै तौ संगि जलै जीवै तौ घरि आंणि ।
जीवण मरणा राम सौं सोई सती करि जांणि ।
3 दादू जाते जीव तैं तौ डरौ जे जिव मेरा होइ ।
जिनि याहु जीव उपाईया सार करैगा सोइ ।
21 माधौदेव उहां हैं आगैं संनमुष आये दरसंन मांगै ।

9A 1 डोलै CG
10A 6 हूं AD BEF
11B 1 आइसु AD BEF ;6 इहि AD BEF
12B 1 ल्यावौ AD BEF
13B 7 तुमही A तुमहि D तुम्है BEF
17A 3 चलैं AD BEF ;6 हूं A हौ D हू BEF
18B 3-4 आज्ञा मैं रहियौ BEF
20A 3-4 बानरा बैसी D बडा रजबैसी BEF
20;3 F

राघौदास र जगिया भाई सादा सेवग अति सुषदाई ।
22 दादूदीनदयाल कौ गंवन सीकरी भाषि ।
जनगोपाल हरि संग रहै कहै संत की साषि ।

Five

1 पहुचे जाई सीकरी पासा तब सुधि पाई भगवंतदासा ।
संनमुष हैं लै गये आई दिन दूवै तीनि करी पहुनाई ।
2 पातिसाह स्यौं कही जु बाता आये स्वांमी सब सुषदाता ।
लाऊं वेगि जु दरसंन पांऊं बोलौ तौ तुमारै घरि आंऊं ।
3 जौ र तुम्हारौ दुवौ पांऊं राजा कह्यौ इहां लै आंऊं ।
स्वांमीहि राजा बात सुनाई अकबर कही सु कहि संमझाई ।
4 स्वांमी कह्यौ कछू हरि आग्या हरिष सोक संसै सब भाग्या ।
तब आतसषांनैं लै जांही पातिसाह कूं जु षबरि सुनांही ।
5 स्वांमी कछू भली सी कहियौ पातिसाह की रूष मै रहियौ ।
नांही कछू जंत्र कौ सारौ राजा रांम बजांवनहारौ ।
1 दादू जे हम छाडैं रांम कौं तौ कौंन गहैगा ।
दादू हम नहीं ऊचरैं तौ कौंन कहैगा ।
6 पातिसाह पठये जंनां तीनी षोटी षरी लेहु तुम चींन्हीं ।
अवलिफजेल बीरबल ग्याता स्वांमी पुछण आऐ बाता ।
7 अरू तहां तीज्यौ तुलसी बांभन रांम छाडि माया कौ रांभन ।
अकबर राइ नमह आवत भाष्यौ स्वांमीं ताकौ मुष न राष्यौ ।
8 जाकौं नवै सकल ही साधा चंद सूर धर पवन आराधा ।
सुर नर सकल करैं जस ताकौ गण गंध्रप गांवैं गुण ताकौ ।
9 नमो निरंजन आत्मरांमां बाबा हंमहि ऐक स्यौं कांमां ।
उपजै बिनसैं आवै जाई झूठे की कहूं कूंण बडाई ।
10 पतिबरता पति स्यौं मंन राषै गंनिका कहां कहां नहीं भाषै
रह्यौ षिसाइ बोल नहीं आवै रांम बिमुष मुष कहा दिषावै ।
11 सेष कह्यौ अब सुनौं गुसांई तुंम हौं बडे हंमारे भांई ।
हंमस्यूं कहौ आपनौं ग्यांनूं कैसौ इष्ट कौंन हैं ध्यांनूं ।
1 दादू स्वरग भवन पाताल मैंधि आदि अंति सब सिष्ट ।
सिरजि सबनि कौं देत है सोई हंमारा इष्ट ।
12 स्वांमीं कहौ इष्ट है सोई जांथैं सब पैंदासि होई ।
ग्यांन हंमारे हरि को नांऊं पंचूं मारि रांम गुंन गांऊं ।
13 सेषु कहै तिहि नांव न ठांऊं उपज्यौ कहां कूंन सैं गांऊं ।
सति सति स्वांमी तब कीनौं सेष र राजाहि ऊतर दीनौं ।
14 जैसौ वहू तैसौ नहीं नांऊं साहिब कह्यौ न जांन्यूं कांऊं ।
सुष कै काज नांव जंन राष्यौ जो गुंन देष्यौ तैसौ भाष्यौ ।

21B 5 चांदा BEF

2B 1 ल्यावहु A ल्यावौ D BEF
14A 2 यहु A वो D वह BEF

15 दया करै तब कह्यौ दयालु गोपाल कहंतां गोपालु ।
घटि घटि रमिता रांम कहावै नांव रहीम रहम थैं पावै ।
16 लह्यौ न जाई अलह कहिये अलषु इहै लेषें थैं रहिये ।
सब सिरजै सो सिरजंनहारू पार न पावैं कहैं अपारू ।
17 मोहन नांव सबनि कौं मोहै सकल बियापी सब मैं सोहै ।
मिश्री कहौ कबै मुष बोली नींब कबै अंतरगति षोली ।
18 ऐसी बिधि यहु नांव बिचार्‌यौ उंनहौं साध बछल धार्‌यौ ।
सब संतनि की सेवा मांनीं प्रगट साषि सकल जगि जांनीं ।
19 राजा सेष बहुत सुष पायौ मांनहु आज परमेसुर आयौ ।
तब सबही बिधि जाई सुनांई पातिसाह मोटी निधि आई ।
20 ऐसौ साध न आयौ कोई अब नांहीं पीछै नहीं होई ।
अकबर कह्यौ जाइ लै आऊ मेरै मंनि दरसंन कौं भाऊ ।
21 सेष र राजा भगवंतदासा तब लै गये अकबर पासा ।
अलह रांम जीव मैं राष्यौ आवहु आऐ ऐसैं भाष्यौ ।
22 साहि अकबर पूछी बाता दादू कहां रहे दिनराता ।
साहिब राषै तहां रहांहीं मंन करि कहूं न आवैं जांहीं ।
23 अब साहिब तुम पै ले आयौ मिटै नहीं जो आप बनायौ ।
सांभरि अरू आंबेरि बताई प्रगटे जहां परमगुरराई ।
24 रहे नजीक मिले क्यूं नांहीं परवांने पुनि आवैं जांहीं ।
जौ तुम कछू बहुत निधि पाई तौ हंमसूं बांटि बांटि किन षाई ।
25 अरू जे कछू जे तुमारै ऊरौ तौ हंमपै थैं करि लेते पूरौ ।
स्वामीं कह्यौ साटि यूं नांहीं कहा करै जलु त्रिषा न मांहीं ।
26 तब पातिसाहि कह्यौ कछू कहिये स्वांमीं कह्यौ बुझि जौ चहिये ।
1 अवलि आब कि बाद प्रकासा प्रथमि जिमी कि भया आकासा ।
पहलां अहरंनि कि भया हथौरा नारि पुरिष का कहिए ब्यौरा ।
2 इनका ऊतर करै जु कोई सोई हमारा मुरसद होई ।
स्वांमी दिल मैं सोच्या सोई समर्थ बिनां न ऊतर होई ।
3 एक सबद मैं सब कीया ऐसा संम्रथ सोइ ।
आगै पीछै तौ करै जे बलहीणां होइ ।
4 तन मटकी मन मही प्रांण बिलोवणहार ।
तत कबीरा ले गया छाछि पीवै संसार ।
घडि ऐक ऐसैं ही जाई तब स्वांमी एक साषि सुनांई ।
27 तन मटकी मन मही प्रांण बिलोवणहार ।
तत कबीरा ले गया औरंनि हूं आधार ।
1 दादू चिडी चंच भरि ले गई नीर निघटि नही जाइ ।
ऐसा बासण नां किया सब दरिया मांहि समाइ ।
2 तब हाथ जोरि अकबरि सिर नाया ऐसा ज्वाब कहीं नहीं पाया ।
षट द्रस्न हम बूझ्या सोई ऐसा ऊतर करै नही कोई ।

24B 4 बौहत C
26A 9 जो C ;B 1-3 अकबर कै मंनि BEF
27 ;1A 2 चाडी B;2B 2 द्रष्म B द्रशण F

28 दादूदीनदयाल सौं कीयौं साहि संबाद ।
जंनगोपाल कहै सुनैं सोई पावै स्वाद ।

Six

1 कहौ बयान अकबर बूझै ज्यूं हंमकौं यामैं निधि सूझै ।
तब स्वांमीं संसय सब षोलै पाइ बसत अकबर बोलै ।
2 क्यूं यहु दसा होई मंन मांहों साधनु थैं गुपता कछु नांहीं ।
मिहरि करौ यहु राह बतावौ सब जीवनि कूं मार्ग लावौ ।
3 दादू इसक महबति मस्त मंन तालिब दर दीदार ।
दोस्त दिल हरदंम हजूरि यादिगार हुसियार ।
4 पहली प्रीति देह स्यौं तोरै ताकै लीये जगत स्यूं जोरै ।
छाडै तीनि लोक की आसा तौ निहचै ब्रह्म करै प्रकासा ।
5 नृपति बीरबल तुलसी भाषी समझे साहि कहा इन राषी ।
तीन्यूं लोक देह मंनु दीजै तब ही जाई रांमरस पीजै ।
6 कीनीं भली देह मंन लाऐ तीन्यूं लोक कहां इन पाऐ ।
इनके भइया कौ घर सोधौ ता पीछैं औरनि परमोधौ ।
7 स्वांमी कह्यौ सुनौं यह बाता ज्यूं हंम छाडे लोक संघाता ।
सिरजंनहार जीव जब कीनौं सब काहू कौं इतनौं दीनौं ।
8 सेर द्वै अंन दोवटी दोई राजा रंकु कोइ किन होई ।
इहि जीव त्रिश्नां बहुत पसारी त्रिपति न होई अचंभौ भारी ।
9 जब है दस तब कहैं बीसा जब है बीस तब सौ की रीसा ।
सहंस लाष तब कहै करोरी ज्यूं ज्यूं बाढै त्यूं त्यूं थोरी ।
10 पहलैं कहै प्रीथमीं पांऊं पीछै कहै सर्गलोक चलि जांऊं ।
इंद्रलोक स्यौं ब्रह्म पतारू इतनौं कब दैहै करतारू ।
11 जब यहु सकल कलपनां जाई तब सब लोक तजे सुनि भाई ।
धंनि धंनि अकबरि भाष्यौ यहु उपदेस न काहु दाष्यौ ।
12 अकबर कह्यौ आपनौं भाऊं दीन के गोष्ठि आइ सुनाऊं ।
स्वांमीं कह्यौ बहुरि नहीं आंऊं परि इकंति लेहिंगे नांऊं ।
13 रहिहौ कहां अकबर भाषै स्वांमी कह्यौ रांम जहां राषै ।
इहि बिधि कथा परसंग सुनायौ अकबर साह कछू दुष पायौ ।
14 सेष कह्यौ अपनैं लै जांऊं गुरबति होइ सु तुंमहि सुनांऊं ।
न्रिपति बीरबल कही जु ऐसी साहि अकबर कैं मंनि बैसी ।
15 पंच राति डेरा ले राषूं गोष्ठि होई सु तुमसुं भाषूं ।
अकबर कहै सेवा बहु कीज्यौ नहीतर हंम कूं सोधौ दीज्यौ ।

2A 7 संतनि A साधनि D साधन BEF
4A 5 तोडै BEF ;10 जोडै BEF
5A 8 इहिं A इनि BEF ;B 1 तीन्यौं AD BEF
7A 10 संगाता AD BEF
8A 7 रांकु C ;B 3 त्रिष्णा AD BEF
10A 3 प्रिर्थी AD BEF ;7 सरगलोक AD, सुर्गलोक G स्वर्गलोक BEF
15B 6 नातरि D नातर B

16 साहि अकबर महलि सिधारे स्वांमीं राजा संगि पधारे ।
राजा वात कही सुषदाई हमहि तुमहि गोब्यंद सगाई ।
17 चलहु चलहु करि बीरा दीनौं राजा कर सूं कर गहि लीनौं ।
महल ठिलायौ दीनौं डेरा अंति नजीक ड्यौढी थैं नेरा ।
18 दिन दूवै राजा कही अनैसी स्वांमीं कै मन मैं नहीं बैसी ।
साच कह्यौ अकबर दुष पायौ पहलै स्वांमीं मंन न मनांयौ ।
19 स्वांमी कह्यौ साच किहि भावै तब राजा जगदीस बतावै ।
स्वांमीं कह्यौ रिझायौ सोई नीकैं बुरें बिचारै कोई ।
20 राजा कह्यौ साहि अवतारू तुमहौं राषौ कछू अधिकारू ।
दरसंन छहूं करत हैं सेवा हींदू तुरक सबनि कौ देवा ।
21 स्वांमी कह्यौ एक ही धांऊं दूजे कौं माथौ नहीं नांऊं ।
कृतम सबै काल बसि भाई केवल ब्रह्म न आवै जाई ।
22 राजा कह्यौ आहि यौ सोई तुमारी द्रिष्टि दूसरौ कोई ।
सेवैं ताहि जू सेवा जांनैं सोइ है तौ बुरौ न मांनैं ।
23 राजा बहुत परछया कीनीं स्वांमी की गति जाई न चींनीं ।
तब थैं कीनीं रांम दुहाई अब कछु फेरि न कहूं बनांई ।
24 चांदा सेवग मंन कौ सूरौ सेवा मांहि रह्यौ मंन पूरौ ।
बहुत भांति स्वांमीं डरपायौ ताकै मंन मैं भै नहीं आयौ ।
25 तब राजा भीतरि पधराऐ दरसंन देषि रांननीं सुष पाऐ ।
देष्यौ मंदिर महल अवासा स्वांमी सब थैं आहि उदासा ।
26 द्रपंनमहल दिषायौ जबही स्वांमी कह्यौ झूठ है सबही ।
झूठी आहि कह्यौ तौ त्यागूं स्वांमी संगि तुमारै लागूं ।
27 स्वांमी कह्यौ झूठ करि जांनूं करि उपगार तजी तैं मांनूं ।
तब स्वांमी डेरा पधराये समाचार पातिसाह सुनाये ।
28 दादूदीनदयाल कौं गोष्टि अंम्रित पांन ।
नृपति बीरबल स्यौं भई जंनगोपाल सु जांन ।

Seven

1 गोष्टि करी द्यौंस चारीसा पार न पांऊं बिसवेबीसा ।
टेक आहि जैसी प्रहिलादू ग्यांन कबीर कहौ भावै दादू ।
2 ध्यांन मंनऊ सुषदेव सरीरा जोग जुगति गोरष थैं नीरा ।
माया मोह नही दुष दंदू जब देषू तब परमांनंदू ।
3 तब पातिसाहि कह्यौ क्या कीजै राजा हमकौं ऊतर दीजै ।
अबकै साहि दरस तुम पांऊं हाथ जोरि अरू माथौ नांऊं ।

17B 2 षुलाइ BEF
22A 4 यहु BE यैहूं F
25A 7 रांनी G रांननि AD रांनींनें B रांनिनि E रांनन F

1A 3 दिवस BEF ;8 बिसवाबीसा AD BEF
2A 2 मनहुं A मानौं D मनौं BEF

4 दीन बोलि ऊनकूं सुष देहू देह दवा माथै करि लेहू ।
दवा फकीरां नजरी षुदाई बेदवा कहर है जाई ।
5 अकबर कह्यौ बेगि लै आऊं हंमहूं देषैं ऊनकौ भाऊं ।
आये राजा सौंध षांनैं कहां करै स्वांमीं कोऊं जांनैं ।
6 पठयौ षोजा स्वांमी पासा राजा बूझै निकटि अवासा ।
आग्या होइ तौ हूं चलि आंऊं पंग धारौ तौ दरसंन पांऊं ।
7 स्वांमीं चले बिलंब न कीनौं जनगोपाल सिष संगि लीनौं ।
जगजीवन डेरां बैठारे स्वांमी राजा पासि पधारे ।
8 आगै आवौ राजा भाषै परमेसुर तुम सरनैं राषै ।
अकबर कही सु बात सुनांई ऊंनकौं दरसंन देहु सुषदाई ।
9 ले राजा दरबार जु आये साहि अकबर ठाढें पाये ।
राजा कह्यौ पधारे दादू पातिसाहि कीनौं संबादू ।
10 रांम न कह्यौ न कीयौ सलांमूं न्रिपष आहि न पष स्यूं कांमूं ।
बातैं कहौ गुसंईयां केरी षीर नीर तुंम्ह देहूं नबेरी ।
11 स्वांमी कह्यौ देह सुधि नांहीं बूझै कहां गुसंईयां मांहीं ।
जौ तुम नहीं गुसंईयां पाये तौ कैसै मैं निकटि बुलाये ।
12 निसदिन करत फिरत बेगारे सहर सीकरी बहुत पिजारे ।
स्वांमी कह्यौ हूतौ संजोगु जैसी बिधि आयौ सब लोगू ।
13 बहु बिधि लोग जगत के आये तिन धूं कहा गुसंईयां पाये ।
साहि अकबर ऐसैं भाषै हंम सूं स्वांमीं अंतर राषै ।
14 जाकै सिरि इतनौं जंजारू ताकूं कहां सिरजनहारू ।
जेती रोम तेती है देहा देहु राह मैं करूं संनेहा ।
15 अपनी दिल कौ साच सूनांऊं जे इहि भांति गुसंईयां पांऊं ।
भले भले स्वांमीं तब भाषै इहि ठां तुम्ही गुसंईयां राषै ।
16 हंमारौ कहिबौ सुनिबौ एहू सदा गुसंईयां यहु गति देहू ।
साहि अकबर माथौ नायौ स्वांमी तुंम दीनौं हंम पायौ ।
1 दवा दिलेसर कौं दई दादू दिल महबूब ।
षैर मिहर मैं राषियौ साहिब तुम्ह कौं षूब ।
17 अब कछू कह्यौ हमारौ कीजै जो चहिये सो हाथैं लीजै ।
स्वांमीं कह्यौ कांम नहीं कोई परमेसुर थैं अंतर होई ।
18 अकबरि कह्यौ लेहू करि भाऊं करौं बंदगी षाहु षुलाऊं ।
स्वांमीं कह्यौ बंदगी सोई आठौ पहर हजूरी होई ।
19 कौंन भांति घर कौं निरबाहू दीनौ लेहू न आप कमाहू ।
अपनै काज करै सब कोई बांटि षाइ संतनि कौं सोई ।
20 कबीर हूं समर्थ का दास हूं कबहूं न होई अकाज ।
पतिब्रता नागी रहै तौ पतिहि कौं लाज ।

4A 3 उनकू AD BEF;B 3 रहम AD BEF
8B 6 उनको AD BEF
9A 1 लै AD BEF
12A 4 निसदिन रहत फिरत भेषधारी सहर सीकरी बहुत भिारी BEF
15A 6 जौ AD BEF

21 सोनौं रूपौ कपरा लीजै सब थोरौ जे तुम्कौं दीजै ।
गांव परगना घोरे हाथी तुम कौ देऊं सुराह संगाती ।
22 फाटैं कपरा भूषैं अंनां हरि धंन सांचैं साधू जंनां ।
पातिसाह पतिसाही छाडै न्रिपति राज तजि आसण मांडै ।
23 कंनक कांमनी संग न लैंही साहिब संनमुष तौ पग दैंही ।
जौ तौं दरब हाथ छुवैं साधू तौतौ लागै अति अपराधू ।
1 सोला सहंस सहेलियां तुरी अठारह लष ।
सांई तेरें कारणैं छोड्या सहर बलष ।
24 कहै अकबर हूं यूं आंनूं लै बाटौ हूं भल मांनूं ।
स्वामीं कह्यौ इतौ अब दीजै सब जीवनि सूं समिता कीजैं ।
25 कौऊं जीव दुष नहीं पावै सिरजंनहार सदा यौं भावै ।
अरू साहिब स्यौं संनमुष रहियौ करि उपगार और स्यौं कहियौ ।
1 तब थैं अकबर जीव न संतायौ प्रम पीर दादू सो पायौ ।
तबही तुरत करी हदीस जीव न संताऊं बिसवाबीस ।
2 जीव दया लीन्हीं है जबही काजी मुलां दूषे तबही ।
काजी मुलां कहैं जु सबही इसकी अजमति लीजै अबही ।
3 काजी मुलां जाइ पुकारे अजमति देषौ हजरति प्यारे ।
सुष न षूब कह्या तुम्ह षासा यहु भी देषैं येक तमासा ।
4 तब अकबर यक कीया स्यंघासन दूजे कूं तहां नांहीं आंसन ।
अजमति देषन की मन मांहीं अबगति की गति जांणौं नांहीं ।
5 अकबरि आसण जाइ बिछाया बीरबल स्वांमी पासि पठाया ।
तब बीरबल या अरज सुणाई स्वांमी मन की लषी सबाई ।
6 कौन काज काहे कौं आया तुम्हैं बुलावन हम है पठाया ।
तब स्वांमी उनके जीव की पाई सकल बारता कहि सुनाई ।
7 अबलिफजल बीरबल दोवैं स्वांमीजी के मुष दिसि जोवैं ।
तब स्वांमी कहै जाइयौ कहियौ हम आये तुम राजी रहीयौ ।
8 सुरति रूप स्वांमी तब कीया जगा सिष संगि करि लीया ।
गैबी मारगि स्वांमी गईया देषि पातिस्याह और अचिरज भईया ।
9 तब आसण अधर आकासि बिराजै नूर तेज सोभा अति राजै ।
तापरि बैठे देषे स्वांमी सकल सिरोमणि अंतरजांमीं ।
10 तबहि अकबर दहसति षाई दादू की गति लषी न जाई ।
तज्यौ सिंघासन करी सलांम तुम मुरसिद मैं गरीबगुलांम ।
11 ऐसौ अदभुत षेल दिषायौ पातिसाह कौ तिमर नसायौ ।
कहै अकबर आसा पूरी मिले षुदाई गये दुष दूरी ।
26 षुसी होई नांइयौ सीसू रहम राषियौ बिसवाबीसू ।
ज्यूं जौहरी नगहि पहचांनैं अरू सराफ नांनैं कूं जांनैं ।
1 काजी मुलां हैरांन देष्यौ आसण कंपे प्रांण ।

21 जै है रसिक रांमरस मांहीं तीनकौं श्रबत मीठौ नांही AC
23B 4 छिवैं BEF
25B 8 अवर BEF
26A 3 करि नायौ BEF ;B 4 पहीचांणत BEF

तुम बकसौ दादू बडे फकीर हिंदू तुरक हूं के पीर ।
27 साहि अकबर बडौ बमेकी षोटी षरी ग्यांन करि देषी ।
विदा होइ स्वांमी पगधारे तब राजा कीनी मनूहारे ।
28 दादूदीनदयाल कौ सुनियौ माया त्याग ।
जंनगोपाल चाहै कोई जौ र लीयौ बैराग ।

Eight

1 अब ज्यूं साहि अकबर राषे ऐक रैनि दिन राजा भाषे ।
स्वांमी कहृयौ ज्यूंही सुष पाऊं मेरेहु मन मैं यहु भाऊ ।
2 तब राजा स्वांमी संगि आये समाचार सेवगनि सुनाये ।
बीती रैनि पहर दिन जाई राजा भीतरि लीये बुलाई ।
3 तहां बहुत भांति बिछौना सोहैं मांनस कहा देवता मोहैं ।
आसन दै राजा बिठारे धंन सु ठौर जहां पगधारे ।
4 स्वांमी ससि राव न्रिप तारे भजन प्रताप जगत उजियारे ।
राजा बिनती कहि समझाई मेरौ कहृयौ करौ सुषदाई ।
5 महुर रुपईयां षिचरी कीन्हीं राजा मांगि थई सो लीन्हीं ।
अरू दस बारह लाये बागे सिषन देहहौं हि जे नागे ।
6 करई राजा चरन पासा त्यूं त्यूं स्वांमीं षरे उदासा ।
स्वांमीं कहृयौ हंमहि सुष देहु तौ लैंन दैंन कौ नांव न लेहु ।
7 रीते वासन मै जल कीजै पूर्ण होइ तौ बाहरि छीजै ।
हरि बिन ठौर नही मंन मांहीं हंम ये महुर कहां ले जांही ।
8 राजा कहृयौ इतौ अब कीजै भलौ मनाई गरीबनि दीजै ।
स्वांमी कहृयौ कौंन की माया और गरीबन कैं के राया ।
9 सबही दिसा बिसंभर पूरै हंमहि न दीसै कहु अधूरै ।
नृमाइल भई राजा यूं भाषै तुंम्ही समरपी अब कौ राषै ।
10 तुंम्ही देहु आपनैं हाथा स्वांमीं कहृयौ चढै जगनाथा ।
राजा बांभन भाट बुलाये अरू गरीब गुरबा तहां चलि आऐ ।
11 स्वांमीं कही दई तिन बांटी बिप्र येक मंनि उपजी आंटी ।
धंनि धनि राजा सुं भाषै नृपति बीरबल मुष नही राषै ।
12 का हंम धंनि कुटंब सब दीनौं तऊं न मंन कौ पूरौ कीनौं ।
स्वांमीं दादू धंनि जू माया त्यागी कलिजुग मांहिं बडे बैरागी ।
1 तब देष्यौ बीरबल बडौ बमेकी तब स्वांमी एक बात बसेषी ।
भली बुधि जांनै सब कोई कहू साहिब हूं मैं महरम होई ।
2 तबहि बरिबलि बीनती दाषी पाग उतरि चरणौं मैं राषी ।
स्वांमी सरम राषियौ मेरी मुझ गंमि नही गुसंईया केरी ।

1A 2 लौं D BEF
2B 5 धाये BEF
3B 3 स्वांमी AD BEF
5A 1 मुहर AD BEF ;B 6 सिर्षानि AD BEF
7A 6 भरिया BEF ;B 9 मुहर D BEF
11A 2 कहृयौ AD BEF

3 तब स्वांमीं मनि करूणा तरी उलटि पाग सीस परि धरी ।
जा सिर तीनि लोक कौ भारूं सरम राषि है सिरजनहारूं ।
4 सिध मिलै सुधि नां मिलै मिलै मिलावै सोइ ।
सूर सिध जब भेटिये तब दुष न ब्यापै कोइ ।
5 गोरषनाथ गली मैं जातें मिहरि करी अति भारी ।
अदब कीया तैं रीझे बाबा हलाल षोरी क्यूं तारी ।
6 यौं बीरबल सौं मिहर जु कीनी भाव भगति की बुधि जु दीनी ।
बीरबल तब दहया लीनी गुर दादू सो पाया चीन्हीं ।
13 राजपाट आपन पौवारूं कछू न कीयौ जिय इहै बिचारूं ।
तब स्वांमी बाहरि उठि आये पीछैं थैं राजा संगि धाये ।
14 रोमांच र गदगद बांनी प्रेमावेस नैंन भरि पांनी ।
फुंन्यं राजा राषे दरबारा पुनरपि दरिस करिहूं किंहि बारा ।
1 भली भई तुम्ह नीक रहे स्वांमी हम सबै सुष लहे ।
सोच बहुत रहता मनि मांही स्वांमी तुम्हसौ हरि का ही ।
2 आगै संत मिले जे कोइ तिनके बहूतक सौदी होई ।
स्वामी तुम कछू अचिरज कीन्हीं अकबर का मन हरि लीन्हीं ।
15 तब राजा भगवंतदास बुलाये भली भई स्वांमीं तुंम्ह आये ।
हमहि अंदेस रैनि दिन भारी हरिजी राषी बात तुम्हारी ।
16 एक रैंनि दिन स्वांमी रहिये भगवंतदास बहुत सुष लहिये ।
1 तब राजा बहु भेट मंगाई स्वामी कहयौ कांमि नही काई ।
भई नृमाइल राजा भाषै तुम्हैं समरपी अब को राषै ।
2 राषौ मिहर करि भेट हमारी तुम्हकौं अरप्यां चटै मुरारी ।
अब राजा कहयौ हमारौ कीजै गरीबनि कौं बांटि यह दीजै ।
3 हुकम करत बांटी तिहि राजा दरब लुटायौ स्वांमी काजा ।
तब राजा कीनी प्रकरमां स्वांमी धनि तुमारौ धरमां ।
निकसि नगर थैं बाहर आऐ चहु दिस संत दरस कौं धाऐ ।
17 जहां जहां स्वांमीं चलि आऐ बहु बिधि संतनि मंगल गाऐ ।
सात बसेरे बन मै बसिये भीड ही डरते गांव न धसिये ।
1 येक ताल परि बैठे आई करौ सनांन स्वामी कहयौ भाई ।
जगै अरज करी सोत बही गरम जलेबी जीमहि अबही ।
2 देषे संत जु भूषे भाई स्वांमी गैब सौ छाब मंगाई ।
सो बरती जो संतनि भाई रही जो दरिया मांहि प्रवाही ।
3 दादूदीनदयाल से सतगुर मिले न कोइ ।
जंगल मैं मंगल कीये सहज महुछे होइ ।
18 गांव औलौदा लाषा नरहरि दास दमोदर जगमत परहरि ।
दूयौसा माह तै लै गये फेरी वहु बिधि भगति करी गुर केरी ।
19 फुंन आये आंबेर मंझारी सब संतनि सुष पायौ भारी ।

14A 5 प्रेमांसु AD BEF ;B 6 दरसन AD BEF
14B 8 कींहिं C कैं A इक BEF
16B 8 साध AD
17A 8 साधनि AD

जिनके कारिज रांम संवारे और कौंन जु आई बिगारे ।
1 इक जोगी बैठि सिला प्रभाई बोल्यौ बचन लियें मंछराई ।
तब टीलै इक बचन प्रकासा जोगी सिला उडे अकासा ।
2 फिरि टीलै करूणा बचन सुणाये तब जोगी सिला धरा परि आये ।
जब जोगी चरन गहे ततकाला अब मोहि राषहु दीनदयाला ।
3 तब स्वांमी के मनि उपजी दया उडता जोगी राषी जु ल्यया ।
उपजी प्रीति सरनि सो आयौ गुर दादू कौ सिष कहायौ ।
20 ल्यायौ तुर्क सगौती रांधी ढाकि ढूंकि कपरा मैं बांधी ।
षांड भांत षोल तातैं देष्यौ दादू साध बडौ करि लेष्यौ ।
21 बूडत हुतौ समद जिहाजा सौदागरि सुमिर्‌यौ तिहि काजा ।
दादू दादू बोल्यौ बांनी अबकै राष्यौ अपनौं जांनीं ।
22 देउं लुटाई षेप यहु आधी अपनै मन मै नीति यूं बांधी ।
तब तिरि लागौ तीरि जिहाजा षेप लुटाइ स्वांमीं काजा ।
23 स्यंन्यासी न मलीदौ षायौ आंबानेरी आइ सुनायौ ।
दींवनगर सब कोइ जांनैं परचो जंनगोपाल बषांनैं ।
1 सात सै साह जिहाज मै बैठे जी सात करोरां माल भर्‌यौ है ।
ताणन पांन लगै काहू कै जाइ समंद्र कै बीचि अरी है ।
2 देस ढूढाहड मांनन रपति राम भगति उहां जु करि है ।
हो रजब साहि पुकार कै नांम जिहाज तिरी है ।
3 एक समैं अैसौ भयौ आई दव्यौ बीरबल हम गिर जाई ।
कासमीर सो दसा कहीजै घाटी भंभर सबद नहि कीजै ।
4 कीन्हौं सोर सुधि नहि पाई गिर्‌यौ हिवारौ धहराई ।
करणा मै कौल बिचार्‌यौ बारन लगी तिहीं छिन तार्‌यौ ।
5 धर्‌यौ हुतौ चरननि मैं सीसा सहाइ बिसवेबीसा ।
जो कोई जीव आसरे आयौ तिन्य तिन्य सबनि प्रेम पद पायौ ।
6 येक समैं कहूं सुरति चलाई अनंत कोटि ब्रह्मंड दिषाई ।
परा सबद अैसै आयौ वारपार काहू अंत नहि पायौ ।
7 आदि अंति आगै रहै येक अनूपम देव ।
निराकार निज निरमला कोई न जाणैं भेव ।
8 अबिनासी अपरपरा वारपार नहीं छेव ।
सो तूं दादू देषि ले उर अंतरि करि सेव ।
ताका भरम काहू विरलै जांनां ।
24 दादू दीनदयाल अग्निनत गुन जग मांहि ।
जंनगोपाल जांनैं जितै कहे सुने ते जांहि ।

20B 4 ताथैं A
22A 9 नीपति AD BEF
23A 1 सिन्यासी A संन्यासनि D BEF
24A 4 अगिनत AD

Nine

1 नट की बाजी कौऊ न जांनैं करता की गति कऊं बषांनैं ।
1 ज्यूं कबीर कै भयौ कमाला ।
त्यूं स्वांमी हूं कै उपजे बाला ।
2 उभै लौंग मृच है दीनी स्वांमी की गति जाइ न चीनी ।
अचिरज बात कही इक भारी ग्रभजती उपजैगे चारी ।
कै स्तुति दांन कि मांनस द्रिष्टी स्वांमीं हूं कै उपजी सिष्टी ।
2 सांभरि गांव समो बतीसा सावन जन्म दीयो जगदीसा ।
दादू पिता प्रगट है जाकै गरीबदास सुत उपज्यौ ताकै ।
3 पंच सात दस बारह बरसूं लागी जात करै सब दरसूं ।
मुनि नारद ज्यूं बेन बजावैं ऊंचै सुरि गंध्रप ज्यूं गावैं । .
4 तुंबर ज्यूं कर गहै जु ताला अंम्रित बांणीं बचन रसाला ।
औरौ गुण नीकैं जग मांही गरीबदास तैं गुप्ता नांही ।
5 ग्रभजती जोबन बैरागी ग्यांन गरीब रह्यौ बिष त्यागी ।
जनगोपाल ताके गुंन गावै और सबनि कें नांव सुनांवैं ।
6 अरू दूजौ भाई मसकीन निसदिन रहै रांम ल्यौलीन ।
स्वांमी की सेवा बहु करई भाव भगति उर अंतर धरई ।
1 स्वांमीजी कौं आग्याकारी भाव भगति सो हिरदै धारी ।
प्रेम प्रीति अरू हरि का ध्यांन जन मसकीन रहै गलतांन ।
2 हरि सुमारण सौं प्रीति अति आठ पहर गलतांन ।
जग ब्यौहार समझै नही अषंड निरंजन ध्यांन ।
7 स्वांमी दादू जाकौ भाई बहन हवा बैरागंनि बाई ।
नांनी माता दोऊं बाई जंनगोपाल यहु कीर्ति गाई ।
8 संतदास गुजराती भाषौं सांगा रांमदास कौं राषौं ।
बूढै देवलिदयालदासूं बैरसल कै हरि बेसासूं ।
9 अरू जैता काइथ गुर भाई स्वांमीं कौं देवल लै जाई ।
स्वांमीं तिनहिं बहुत सुष दीनौं जैजैकार सकल जुग कीनौं ।
10 आवत जात रांम गुंन गाये फिरि स्वांमीं आंबेरि जु आये ।
बरस ऐक बीतौ है जबही रमिबे कौ समयौ भयौ तबही ।
11 नरहरदास रू माधौ कांनी लीला करी टौंक जग जांनी ।
हठू करि स्वांमीं कु लहि जांहीं आये संत अंत कहूं नांहीं ।
12 अंधियार बाग भयौ बाजारू दरस काज उमह्यौ संसारू ।
ताल पषावज मंगल गावैं स्वांमी कौ दरसंन सब पांवैं ।
1 समगरी थोरी कुछ जांनीं स्वांमी पूछे माधौ कांणीं ।
तब स्वांमीं कह्यौ सोच मति आंनौं अंत्रजांमी निकटि जांनौं ।
2 भरि थारी पकवान हि ल्यायौ तब स्वांमी हरि कौ भोग लगायौ ।
प्रसादी लै गंज मैं राषी भयौ अटूट संत सब साषी ।

1A 4 कोउ A कोई D कोऊ BEF ;10 कौंन AD BEF
4B 8 दुरलभ AD BEF
8A 4 मांगा AD BEF
9B 2 ताकौं D ;6-10 सब संतनि मिलि दरसन कीनैं AD BEF

3 तब टीलै अरज स्वांमी सौ करी प्रसादी कौ अति अरबी परी ।
अरू यह अचारी हम बिचारी लई प्रसादी हठ करि भारी ।
4 कौंन कला येहू बरती स्वांमी टीला पूछै अंत्रजांमीं ।
चम द्रष्टि सब केरी करता इनकी बुधि यूं फेरी ।
5 लीला राजा रांम की षेलै सबही संत ।
आपा पर येकै भया छूरी सभै भरंत ।
6 पूरणब्रह्म प्रगटे आदू सब कोऊ चाहै प्रसादू ।
तिन आत्म कौ देषि सनेहा स्वांमी तिन नीधारी देहा ।
7 दीनदयाल दया मनि आई दीन्हीं लौंग सबनि मनि भाई ।
संम्रथ करै कहा नहीं होई अबिगति लषै न कोई ।
8 तब माधौ पूछै अधिकारी सब जीवन के हित प्रउपगारी ।
मुठी चारि लौंग मुकलाये सो सबहनि कैसैं आये ।
9 अंत्रजांमीं कीया पसाव जाकौ जैसौ देष्यौ भाव ।
पांच षष्ट अरू सात बसेषे माधौ लौंग सबनि पै देषे ।
10 दुती भाव दुबिध्या मिटी सुषी कीये सब संत ।
टौंक महोछे कारणैं दादू भये अनंत ।
11 सुरति रूप सरीर का पीव के प्रसें होइ ।
दादू तन मन येक करस सुमिरण कहिये सोइ ।
13 सात दिवस लीला तब कीनीं स्वांमीं चले बिदूया तिनि दीनीं ।
गुढिला कूं स्वांमीं पगुधारे बालिक सेवग संगि सिधारे ।
14 पथ चलत गांईन तहां घेरे बहुति निमैं स्वांमीं तिनि हेरे ।
सब गांइनि मिलि मंडल कीनौं ठाढे रहि स्वांमी सुष दीनौं ।
15 ज्यूं ज्यूं चलैं त्यूं हि संगि धावैं ठाढे रहैं तो सीस नवांवैं ।
सब संतनि मिलि अचिरज कीनौं स्वांमीं इनकौ मनु हरिलीनौं ।
1 दादूदीनदयालजी दया करी तहां आइ ।
जनगोपाल संसा नहीं मुकति करी सब गाइ ।
16 नटवारे है गुढिला आऐ भगत दमोदर अति सुष पाऐ ।
कियौ मिलाप दूयौंस दूवै तीनीं भाव भगति बहुत विधि कीनीं ।
17 स्वांमीं फिरि आऐ आंबैरी अरथ दैई न काहू फेरी ।
बीते जबहि दूयौंस दूवैं तीनी सेवग मिलै रू बिनती कीनीं ।
18 स्वांमीं कृपा करौ पगधारौ हंम जीवनि के कारिज सारौ ।
पूर्णदास महाजन आंधी तजि संसारू रांम ल्यौ बांधी ।
19 बहुत बार स्वांमीं तहां आये किऐ महोछे मंगल गाये ।
फुंनि जैमल जोगी संभराई स्वांमी कौ सेवग सुषदाई ।
20 जब स्वांमीं उनकै घरि जांई छाजू भाइ अंगि नमांई ।
हरीदास रांणां अरू मोहन सेवग सब जैमल के गोहन ।

13A 4 तहां AD BEF
14A 9 तहां A BEF;B 4 मंगल A
17A 5 आग्या AD BEF ;B 3 मास D बरस BEF
19A 2 बेर AD BEF
20B 2 हरसिंघ AD ;B 9 अतिसोहन D

21 तिनकौं सुष दे स्वांमीं आये सबही संतनि के मंनि भाये ।
अरू चाटसू कपिल है नीकौ अध्यात्म जांनैं जग फीकौ ।
22 स्वांमीं कौ सिष्य मंनि भायौ ठाटि महौछौ लैंन सु आयौ ।
स्वांमी तिनहुं बहुत सुष दीनौं जैजैकार सकल जुग कीनौं ।
23 मिल्यौ बागरौ तोल्हौ आई छाडी लज्या लोक बडाई ।
परमेसुर कौ भलौ मनांवैं हिंदू तूरक न काहू भावै ।
24 अरू आंबैरि भये बैरागी लालदास सेवग मंति जागी ।
सेवग केसौ बधू र दूजंन चरन कंवल स्वांमीं के पूजंन ।
25 मोहनदास भये बैरागी पटंन तैं माया संगु त्यागी ।
लालदास नाईक संगि आयौ स्वांमीजी कौ दरसंन पायौ ।
26 प्रागदास झाझू भगवांनूं हरीदास गोपाल सुजांनूं ।
मोहनदास भलौ मेवारौ स्वांमीं कौ सिष सब गुंन सारौ ।
27 दादूदीनदयाल की लीला अगम अपार ।
जंनगोपाल जपिबो करै निसदिन बारबार ।

Ten

1 बहुत दूयौंस बीति जब जांहीं करता करै सु मिटै नांहीं ।
मांनस्यंघ आंबैरि पधारयौ मिलिबे कौं सब जग सिधारयौ ।
2 मिले मनोहरपूरन अचलौरू मिले रांमगढ जौ जिहि ठौरू ।
मिले गोरिवै डेरां मांही स्वांमी बिनां रह्यौ कोऊं नांही ।
3 बीते जबहि दूयौंस द्वै तीनी सब लोगनि मिलि चुंगली कीनी ।
राजा दादू कै अभिमांनूं मांनैं नहीं तुम्हारी आंनूं ।
4 और करै अंनीती अैसी राजा पुछ्यौ कहौ न कैसी ।
हीदू तूरक ऐक जिहि कीनौं बांभन बनियां संमि करि लीनौं ।
5 चारि बरन कौ रह्यौ भेदू झूठौ पर्यौ तुमारौ बेदू ।
मुई त्रिया जगलि मैं छाडी क्रिया करी न भौंइ मैं गाडी ।
6 राषी नही येकहू राहा हीदू तूरक दोऊं जिहि बाहा ।
बेटा बेटी कंवारे राषे आति अपराध बेद मैं भाषे ।
7 सात बरस लौं कन्यां कहिये बारह नांव सु बेटी लहिये ।
सोलह कौं तब रहै न धर्मूं होई बीस की आहि अकरमूं ।
8 देस दोष कै लागै राजा किनि संमझाई कहौ तिंहि काजा ।
राजा स्वांमी मिले बुलाई मिले प्रीति सूं बात चलाई ।
9 पहलैं मिले रांम गढ मांहीं राजा कह्यौ भूलि नही जांहीं ।

24B 1 चेतनि AD BEF
25A 7 सब A संग D जिनि BEF

1A 6-10 भगवंत स्यंघ हरि मांहि समांही BEF
3A 9 चुगली AD BEF
3B 8 कांनी D कानौ BEF
5B 1-2 मरै ताहि BEF ; 9 भुइ D भ्वै A भ्व BEF
8B 3 लांये A लिये D कै चलि BEF

हंम स्वांमी महिमांन तुम्हारा पूछी नहीं हमारी सारा ।
10 स्वांमीं कह्यौ सार हंम बूझी परमेसुर आग्या जो सूझी ।
तब राजा पूछी यहु बाता सुन्यौं रांम की छाड़यौ गाता ।
11 सो तुम्ह लै गाड कै जारी तब स्वांमी दूवै साषि बिचारी ।
साध सूर सोहैं मैदांनां तिनकूं नांहीं गोर मसांनां ।
12 कबीर मरण तहां जौ पाइयों जहां आपणां न कोई ।
अहंमष भषैं जनांवरां बात न बूझै कोई ।
13 हरि भजि साफिल जीवणां पर उपगार समाई ।
दादू मरणां तहां भला जहां पसु पंषी षाई ।
14 बेटी बेटनि की मंन मांही राजा बूझि सकै सो नांहीं ।
स्वांमी हूं कै सिरी धरि बूझी महापुरिष अंतरगति सूझी ।
15 अब स्वांमी करिहौ नही ब्याहू तरन सरीर के सब स्याहू ।
स्वांमी कह्यौ ग्यांन अति थोरै माता पिता करांहै भोरै ।
1 विषै बिकार जरै जग सोई सीलवंत का दोष न कोई ।
तब राजा मन मैं डरप्यौ भारी स्वांमी मन की जांनैं सारी ।
2 कबीर नरनारी सब नरक है जब लग देह सकांम ।
कहै कबीर ते रांम का जे सुमिरै निहकांम ।
16 हंम सब त्रिया रांम भरतारू ता बिन सब दीसै बिभचारू ।
कूंन ग्यांन घट सूं घट जोरैं भांडे सूं भांडौ गहि फोरैं ।
17 लै नारीनर कै गलि बांधै नर की सुरति त्रियां सूं सांधै ।
यूं हरि बिसर्यौं बिसवाबीसैं ताथैं हंम कूं अनरथ दीसैं ।
18 बांभन बनियां न्रिप बलिषंडा सात बरस की हूंहि जु रंडा ।
1 बिषै कौं मन उठि भागै इनकौ दोष कौंणकौं लागै ।
ते क्यूं रहैं लोक की लाजा परमेसुर सूं नांहीं काजा ।
गरभगल्यां की हत्या होई दोष देस कौं लागै सोई ।
2 येक ब्रह्म कौ सदा बिचारा सील साच कौ है अधिकारा ।
धरि बेसास रू भजन करांहीं इनकौ तुमकौं दोष सु नांहीं ।
19 धंनि धंनि भाषै सब कोई यौहु अपराध कौन कूं होई ।
हंम नहीं करैं न बरजै काऊं बिष अंम्रित भावै सो षाऊ ।
20 सोई माइ सास पुनि सोई सोई घर की नारी ।
कहै कबीर परंम पद पाया संतौ लेहु बिचारी ।
21 बहन बीर सब देषिये नारी अरू भरतार ।
परमेसुर के पेट का दादू सब परिवार ।
22 स्वांमी कही स राजा भाई सिष साषनि की बात चलाई ।
कौंन सिष कौ आवै जाई स्वांमी तुम कू अंतरू नांहीं ।
23 स्वांमी कहै मैं न सिष कीनां अपनैं भाई भये लैलीनां ।

12B 1 आमष BEF
14B 1-6 डरतौ राजा सकै न बूझी BEF
15A अब स्वांमी संसै सब षोलै कर जोरै राजा नहीं बोलै BEF
15B स्वांमी कह्यौ सुणौं अब राजा कीयौ मनोरथ तैं बेकाजा BEF
18A 4 बलिषंडा AD बलषंड BEF

जैसें चंद कमोदनि जांनैं ज्यूं भूजंग चंदन पहिचांनैं ।
24 ज्यूं अकास रवि कवलहि बूझै ज्यूं पतंग पतंग कूं सूझै ।
ज्यूं बोहिथ काहूं न बुलावै पार उतारै जौ चढि आवै ।
25 आवै संत सवै दिस चारी राजा रांम करे रषवारी ।
हरदी चूंनौं मिलि रंग होई प्रेम सनेही मिलिहि जौ दोई ।
26 षांन पांन कैसी बिधि होई रोक न लेहु कमाइ न कोई ।
अति ऊंचे तनि बस्तर सोहैं बहुत साध तुंम संगति जोहै ।
27 कबीर जीवत म्रितक है रहै तजै जगत की आस ।
तब हरि सेवा आपन करै मति दुष पावै दास ।
28 दादूदीनदयाल सूं मांनस्यंघ संबाद ।
जनगोपाल जांनैं नहीं सो क्यूं पावै स्वाद ।

Eleven

1 टीला सिष्य हुतौ तब संगा मांनस्यंघ पूछ्यौ परसंगा ।
भली भांति ऊतर तिंहि दीनौं मिटि उपाधी इहै मतु कीनौं ।
1 टीलै सबद ऐसौ इक कह्यौ मनसिंघ चुपकौ है रह्यौ ।
राजा देषौ सोचि बिचारी रांम नांम बिन सबै षुवारी ।
2 राजा कौ मंन देष्यौ नीकौ तब ही बीप्रनि मुष कीयौ फीकौ ।
राजा कह्यौ अनमंनें काहे महाराजि दादू अंति दाहे ।
3 ऐतौ मिले रांम कूं जाई हमारै बेद मैं नही चलि आई ।
अरू राजा दादू कौ थापैं तौ दादूपंथी सब को आपै ।
4 तब राजा मंन कीयौ बिचारू हंम थैं दूरि रह्यौ करतारू ।
अर जे देही दुनि कूं छाडी तौ एकौ बात न आवै आडी ।
1 बिप्रन का क्या बिगरै भाई राजा रीति भिष्ट है जाई ।
अरू जे संतनि कौ दुष दीजै अपजस होइ अर नरक परीजै ।
5 राजा जीवन भाव कुभाऊ साध बडौ भल रहौ कि जाऊ ।
तब राजा बरसन की बूझी भये किते दिन तुमकौं सूझी ।
6 बरस चवदह स्वांमी भाषै सिरजंनहार जहां अब राषै ।
स्वांमीं उठे डरे तब राजा संत दूषायौ मैं बेकाजा ।
1 मैं नहीं जांनूं तुम उठि जास्यौ मैं तौ बचन सहजि प्रकास्यौ ।
चूक हमारी वकसौ स्वांमीं मैं तुम जांनें अंतरजांमीं ।
7 स्वामी कह्यौ डरे जिनि राजा करिहै रांम तुमारे काजा ।
हरि है बीचि हम तुम मांहीं भलौ बुरौ बाछै कछू नांहीं ।
8 तुंम हो साध वडे मैं जांनूं दूष्ट लोक गति कहा बषांनूं ।
1 जब स्वामी ऊठन की धारी तब प्रमेस्वर कोप्यौ भारी ।
पीछै सवद भयौ आकासा दादू बोलि करौं सब नासा ।
2 तब स्वांमी मनि करूणा करी ।

23B 7 दीपक A

1B 7 उपाधि A BEF
7A 4 मति A BEF

ऐ सब जीव उबारौ हरी ।

3 आत्म जीव अनाथ सब करतार उबारै ।
राम निहोरा कीजिये जिनि काहू मारै ।

4 नारद कोप्यौ संत बिन कोपि कह्यौ इक बैंन ।
नगरी उबरी संत सरणि बजर सिला तैं चैंन ।

5 यूं साहिब कोप्यौ यौ भारी परलै करतौ नगरी सारी ।
तब स्वांमी हरि सौं बीनती कीनीं आंबानेरी राषि जु लीनीं ।

6 तब राजा कौं कुछ चेटक भईया तुरतहि आइ चरन जब गहिया ।
अबहौं जांण न देहूं स्वांमी रहौ कृपा करि अंत्रजांमीं ।

7 मांनस्यंघ जब नायौ माथा तब स्वांमी सिष राष्यौ जगनाथा ।
दूवारौ कीयौ ताल की तीरा पीछैं बाग निकट ही नीरा ।

8 तब राजा मन मैं सुष पायौ कछू इक दिन स्वामी ठहरायौ ।
राजा कौं तब धीरज दीनीं पीछैं स्वांमीं रांमति कीनीं ।
तब स्वांमीं घर आई लुटायौ कपराचुपरा अंन बटायौ ।

9 स्वांमीं बैरागी पगधारे मांनस लै सेवग जु सिधारे ।
दिन पांच मारग मैं लागे रहे भुरभुरे संत सभागे ।

10 राघौदास जु सेवा कीनी स्वांमीं तहां रहे मास तीनी ।
कल्यांणपुर पीथा न्रिबांनूं जांनै भाव गति परवांनूं ।

11 संगति सदा रूप बैरागी सांमी के दरसंन मति जागी ।
दरसंन काजि भुरभुरै आयौ चलहु उहां मैं सरबसु पायौ ।

12 बहुत भांति सूरातंन कीनौं लोक लाज भै मन नहीं दीनौं ।
फुंनि स्वांमी कल्यांणपुर आयौ सुनि हरि रांम बहुत सुष पायौ ।

13 रहे बरस दिन फुंनि पगुधारे पछिम दिसा रमि दिन चारे ।
षेलत रमत गये तब पादू सेवा करी टकू गुर दादू ।

14 माधौदास जु लैंन षंदाऐ लै मोहन रेयां तहां आऐ ।
कीरतन सुंनि दरसंन पायौ माधौदास प्रेम मन भायौ ।

15 नरबद रहै ईंडवै थांनूं राजस तजै भजै भगवांनूं ।
स्वांमीजी कौ दरसंन पायौ भगति करी बहु प्रेम बढायौ ।

16 किस्नस्यंघ राठौर हि जांनूं स्वांमी कौ सेवग परवांनूं ।
तिलांने स्वांमी पधराये कीये उछाह बहुत मनि भाये ।

17 रैवंत संत दास जु पिजारौ भलौ साध प्रमेसुर प्यारौ ।
भाव भगति प्रेम अति भारी स्वांमी ताकी प्रीति बिचारी ।

18 रांनीं गांऊ जु राघौदासू उदासुत कै हरि बेसासू ।
भाव भगति सेवा बहु कींनीं काहु जाइ राव सुधि दीनी ।

19 सात गांव छाडे कछवाहै परमेसुर कौ ब्रत निबाहै ।
मांनिसिघ राठौर भवादी स्वांमी कौं सिष सतवादी ।

20 राघौदास जाति चौहांनूं तोसीनैं सेवग प्रवांनूं ।
प्रिथीराज आहि लघु भाई स्वांमीजी स्यूं प्रीति बढाई ।

10A 8 दिन A BEF
16A 2-3 ताकौ सुत BEF ;5-8 रजधांनी मेडता जाकै BEF
18B 3 लीला BEF

21 तिनकैं रहैं कछू दिन स्वांमीं गुर सेये ज्यूं अंतरजांमीं ।
दादूदीनदयाल की लीला अगम अगाध ।
जंनगोपाल जपिबो करै प्रमेसुर अरू साध ।

Twelve

1 बीकानेरि भुरटिया राऊं स्वांमीं सुन्यौ देस मैं आऊं ।
तिहिं षादू थैं बेगि बुलाऐ स्वांमी दादू तिहि ठाहर आऐ ।
2 तोसीनैं थैं लीऐ बुलाई स्वांमी की गति लषै न काई ।
कौंन धर्मु कौंन है रहनीं कहां करतूति कहा है कहनीं ।
3 रांम नांम निज ध्रंम हंमारै रहनि इहै जे पंचूं मारै ।
अरू करतूति जु संतनि कीनीं नींकी इहै रांम ल्यौलीनीं ।
4 ताके मन मैं कथा न आई स्वांमी कह्यौ धीजं करि भाई ।
ग्यांन नही सब राई भाषी तायैं संतनि कथा न राषी ।
5 मातौ हाथी द्वारै राष्यौ तब स्वांमी सूं डेरा भाष्यौ ।
स्वांमीं गज संनमुष चलि जांहिं गरीबदास तब पकरी बांहीं ।
6 ईनकौ भाव भलौ कछू नांहीं आंन बाट है डेरा जांहीं ।
ईनकौ भाव जु इनकूं होइ हंमकूं राषै संम्रथ सोई ।
7 गरीवदास सुरातंन कीनौं रजब कर कर सूं गहि लीनौं ।
स्वांमी कै संगि निकसे दोइ देषि राव मन अचिरज होइ ।
8 हाथी रह्यौ ठग्यौ सौ ठाढौ मानौं लिष्यौ चित्र कौ गाढौ ।
टीला संगि बैरागी आये स्वांमीं कौ पीछौ गहि धाये ।
9 तब दुर्गौं अपनैं लै जाई भाव भगति सेवा सुषदाई ।
दूजै स्वांमी राव बुलाऐ तब ही माला तिलक सुनाऐ ।
10 सब कोई मोस्यूं यौं भाषै ऐक सुमिरणीं स्वांमी राषै ।
काठ नहीं कंचन की देऊं हूं सुष पाई चरन नितां सेऊं ।
11 स्वांमी कह्यौ तिलक है सोई मन माला गुरि दीनीं पोई ।
कंचन काठ नहीं कोई कांमां जिनि कौ हिरदै आत्मरांमां ।
12 कबीर माला काठ की कहि संमझावै तोहि ।
मन न फिरावै आपनां कहा फिरावै मोहि ।
13 दादू सतगुर माला मंन दीया पवन सुरति सूं पोई ।
बिन हाथूं निसदिन जपै परम जाप यूं होई ।
14 राव कहैं रहौ नगर हंमारै लावौ मांनस सेवग द्वारै ।
सेवा करूं घर करवांऊं बरज्यूं भीर दरसहूं पांऊं ।
15 स्वांमीं कह्यौ कहैंगे तैसी करि बिचार अंतरगति जैसी ।
बिदा होइ डेरा तब आये समाचार सेवगनि सुनाये ।
16 स्वांमीं सेवग बात विचारै संत न हूंहि पराऐ सारै ।
तीजैं राव बुलाऐ जबहीं सांची बात कहीं हैं तबहीं ।

2A 1 षबरि सुने A BEF
11B 9 हरि हे रांमां A अंत्रजांमी BEF
16A 5 साध A BEF

17 राषे रांम रहैंगे त्यूंहीं राजा परजा कोऊ क्यूंहीं ।
पहल्ल बुलाए भाव करि पीछैं कीयौ कुभाव ।
औरनि कौ बाह्यौ बह्यौ ताथैं भोरौ राव ।
1 स्वांमी सुषन असौ तब कहियौ राज तेज तबही तैं गईयौ ।
जब कोई गार्दा बैठै आई राज तेज मद उतरि जाई ।
18 तोर्सानैं है स्वांमीं आए दूबारै सेवग तिनि सुष पाए ।
अरू जब बीते समए दोई ढूंढाहर की बीनती होई ।
19 स्वांमी गए सबनि सुष पाए जौ लै है दूबारै तब आए ।
बरस एक बीत्यौ है जबहीं लाडषांन पधराए तबही ।
20 न्यौलावांसायैं ईसर कछवाहौ सेवग सूरौ ब्रत निबाहौ ।
त्रिया पुरिष की मिटी सगाई रहै समिप बहन ज्यूं भाई ।
21 ता पीछैं घाटवै पधारे लाडषांन सेए दिन बारे ।
भाव भगति महौछौ कीनौं स्वांमी चले पयांनौं दीनौं ।
22 पीछैं प्रागदास ले चले जाति महाजंन सिष सुभले ।
किरडौली कौं कियौ पयानौं बीच साहिपुर भयो मिलांनौं ।
23 साहि तिलोक आहि सिकदारू स्वांमीं के दरसंन सूं प्यारू ।
कोस एक थैं लै गयौ जु फेरी बहु बिधि भगति करी तिन केरी ।
24 बहुत भांति भोजंन करवायौ कथा कीरतनु अंति सुष पायौ ।
स्वांमीं उठि परभाति पधारे अरू समीप के संग सिधारे ।
1 साह तिलोक कै उपजी मन मांहीं प्रचा कोऊ देष्यौ नांहीं ।
तब स्वांमीं वाकौ हिरदौ जीयौ साह तिलोक कौं संसौ षोयौ ।
25 साहु तिलोक जु लियौ बुलाई सौंज संभालि कालि जौ आई ।
सौरि पालिके और पिछौरा बिछावने जाजम तिहिं ठौरा ।
26 षैंच्यौ आइ पिछौरा जबही स्वांमी बैठे देषे तबहीं ।
तब तिहि बोलि लिए ढिग औरा स्वांमी ऐकि धू हैं ऊहि ठौरा ।
27 बाहरि भीतरि दरसंन देष्या जीवन जन्म सुफल करि लेष्यौ ।
तिहि स्वांमीं सूं बीनती कीनीं स्वांमीं तुम्ह गति जाइ न चीनीं ।
1 साहि तिलोक फैंटा जब दीया तब स्वांमी हुकम साह कौं कीया ।
तब स्वांमी यक कला दिषावै फेटै मांहि बधणीं नहीं आवै ।
2 तब साह तिलोक अचंभौ आंनैं स्वांमी सब के मन की जांनैं ।
उभै ठौर देष्यौ दीदार तब साहि तिलोक कै भयौ करार ।
28 स्वांमी कह्यौ ऐक तन मेरौ भाव तुम्हारौ तुम्ह थैं नेरौ ।
स्वांमी तब किरडौली आए प्रागदास सेवग सुष पाए ।
1 परि अतीत कौ प्रचौ नहीं लीजै सरधा सारू सेव सु कीजै ।
साह तिलोक सेवा बहु कीन्हीं परि स्वांमी की गति जाइ न चीन्हीं ।
29 दादूदीनदयाल की लीला अगम अनंत ।
जंनगोपाल जंपिबो करै जुगि जुगि दादू संत ।

17A 6 रांना A
20A 1 नौलासे A न्यौलासे BEF
22A 2 पिरागदास A BEF
24A 3-4 करि भाव बटायौ EEF

Thirteen

1 स्वांमी कौ सेवग मंन भायौ गोपालदास लैंन तहां आयौ
जाति महाजन हरि कौ दासूं बसै गांव डिडवांनैं बासूं ।
2 बहुत भांतिहि कीयौ उछाहूं भाव भगति भावै सब काहूं ।
चारयूं दिसा दरसन कौं आवैं अधिकारी सब दरसन पावैं ।
3 पाच द्यौंस लीला तहां कीनीं स्वांमी चले बिदा सब दीनीं ।
अरू गोपाल जोईसी नागोरी रामदास कैं प्रीति न थोरी ।
4 रोद्र मांहि महाजन सारन स्वांमी मिलै रह्यौ हरि कारन
बहुत भांति संतनि सुष दीनौं तबहि गवन द्वारै कौं कीनौं ।
5 तीनि मास द्वारै रहै मारवारि फुनि जांहि ।
अरसपरस साधु मिलै अनभै तीरथ न्हांहि ।

1 ख्वाजा सौं आयौ दरवेसा दोई वस्त तहां कीन्हीं पेसा ।
दोना मांहै मिसरी फूल सो स्वांमीं नहीं करी कबूल ।
2 आध घरी जब बीती जाई पंच पतासे लीये मंगाई ।
स्वांमीजी आग्या जब दीनीं उठि मारग अपना लीया चीन्हीं ।
3 अंत्रजांमीं सब की जांनैं आंन वस्त सौं निकसैं कांनैं ।
जाकौ ले करि ताहि चढाई स्वांमीं कहै निधि गुपता पाई ।
4 संता कह्यौ सुनौ जी स्वांमी हम नहीं समझै अंत्रजांमीं ।
स्वांमीं कहै भेट इहां नहीं चहिये साहिब दे सोई कर गहिये ।
5 तब ख्वाजे पीर स्वांमी पै आया हस्त जोरि अर सीस नवाया ।
तुम दादू धनि करतार रिझायौ मांगि पिरांनीं हम पछितायौ ।
6 अप्रछन पीरि बीनती लाई हम सौं मिहर करौ सुषदाई ।
स्वांमीं सनमुष आये ख्वाजा तुम्हैं मिले अबिनासी राजा ।
7 हमै तुम्हैं बिचि अंत्र येता जौंगिनैं सूरज जांनौं तेता ।
सूरजरूपी तुम्ह हौ स्वांमी हूं जुगिनौं माया सहकांमीं ।
8 स्वांमी कहै तुम्ह सौं मिहर गुसया कीन्हीं सब आतम तुम्ह आगैं दीन्हीं ।
हम ऐक गुसंईयां और न चांहै सो हरिजी हम तुम्ह मांहै ।
9 साहिब बिनां न मांगैं दूजा सबै अक्यारथ आनै पूजा ।
पीर औलिया सिधि क्यूं पाई हरि की दीन्हीं लहीं बडाई ।
10 करी बंदगी साहिब आगै आतम द्यौ दूरि हम सौं लागै ।
दुनियां का सुष मांग्या ऊरा उनसौं रांम रहे कहीं दूरा ।
11 संकट मैं सब लोक बडाई पीरूं की फुनि इहै बडाई ।
उठ सिधि नौ निधि हरि की चेरी संत रहे तिनसौं मुह फेरी ।

6 सिष ऐक रजब अधिकारी ग्यांनी गुनीं सूर अति भारी ।
ग्रभ जती होते बैरागी स्वांमी के दरसन करि त्यागी ।
7 ताके मन मैं उपज्यौ भाऊ करूं महोछौ स्वांमीं आऊ ।
बहुत भांति करि रिझये स्वांमीं हमकूं सांचौ अंतरजांमीं ।
8 बहुत भांति करि बीनती कीनी तब चलिबे की आग्या दीनीं ।

3 A 7-8 तिनहि अभौगति BEF
5 ;5B 7 प्यरांनी E

पांच सात दिन मैं चलि जांहीं सींचे संत जु आऐ मांहीं ।
9 बोहिथ षेमदास अरू टीकौ षेतौ टोहौ गोब्यंद द्वौ नीकौ ।
अल्हन्यावास पधारे स्वांमीं सब मिलि पूजे अंतरजांमीं ।
10 कारू मैं घडसी बैरागी माया मोह रह्यौ सब त्यागी ।
ताके कुटंब महोछौ कीनौं तेहु अपनौं श्रबसु दीनौं ।
11 तब आए केवलपुर ठांऊं दौरे संत सुने जिहि नांऊं ।
भगति महोछौ लीला भारी संतोषे रजब दिन चारि ।
12 राघौ गोब्यंद और नरांइन रजब के सिष भगति परांइन ।
ठाकुरदास तहां लै जांई नील्या मैं जिहि जुगति बनांई ।
13 अरू आयौ तहां गोइंददासा दरसन पायौ पूर्जा आसा ।
भाव भगति महौछौ कीनौं स्वामी तिनहि बहुत सुष दीनौं ।
14 पादू तब स्वांमी पगधारे सेव्रग टाकू के कारज सारे ।
केसौ कौ कानईया तहां आयौ स्वांमी कौ दरसन तिहि पायौ ।
1 जल प्रसाद आल्हण कौं दीयौ प्रेम प्रीति सूं आल्हण लीयौ ।
बाहरि भीतरि भयौ प्रकासा आल्हणि पायौ प्रम निवासा ।
2 करामाति आल्हण की भई उभै मास की पाडी दुही ।
ताकौ अचिरज मांनै बात आल्हण की तब लागी जात ।
15 संगि जसवंत और जगनाथा दरसै चारण पूछी गाथा ।
औतारन की बात चलाई स्वामी कही हमहि समझाई ।
16 स्वामी कह्यौ आदि है जाकौ पीछै अंत होइगै ताकौ ।
दूवै गुण थैं परमेसुर न्यारौ तुमही मन मैं ग्यान बिचारौ ।
17 दादू क्रितम नही सो ब्रह्म है घटै बधै नहीं जाई
निहिचल पूरन येक रस जगति न नाचै आई ।
18 गांव पालरी जाकौ बासू नीकौ सेवग कान्हरदासू ।
सकल भरम तजि सरनै आयौ स्वांमी की संगति सचु पायौ ।
19 दूजण साध ईडवा मांही निकटि सरोवर हरि की छांहीं ।
गुर कौ सदा रसोईदार बैरागी दूजण गुणसार ।
20 रूपा जीता लषू र बाई राइमल हांमां सुषदाई ।
नरबद कौ बाघ अति नीकौ भलौ मनायौ स्वामीजी कौ ।
21 तिनकौं सुष दे स्वांमी आऐ सबही संतनि मंगल गाऐ ।
पीछै रहे कछू दिन दूवारै साहिब की आग्या पगधारै ।
22 राइ सिंघ कछवा हौ जांनौं स्वामी कौ सेवग प्रवांनौ ।
त्यौंधि महोछौ कीनौं भारी भाव भगति हरि प्रीति बिचारी ।
23 दूढाहर के सेवग आऐ बीनती करि स्वांमी पधाऐ ।
प्रथम कहूं सेवग बैरागी जिनकी प्रीति प्रम गुर लागी ।
24 येकत स्वांमी दूवारै राषे संगि चले जु कथा मैं भाषे ।

8B 7-11 आये संत अंत कहू नांहीं BEF
9A 2 रामदास BEF ;4-8 तीकौं गोब्यंद षेतौ षरथर BEF
10A 1 काल्हू BEF
14A 6 ढकूं B
19A 2 दूजनदास BEF

बडौ गोपाल रू सींधू पीपा चंदा बाला रहै समीपा ।
25 केसौ अरू बाबा भगवांनूं माधौ संतदास प्रवांनूं ।
सिष मोहन दफतरी बांचौ हरि गुन लिषे रे गुर सूं सांचौ ।
26 पीपा बंसी परमांनंद्र किस्नदास कै मनि आंनंद्र ।
कोरी मोनी दयाल बंगाली साधू देवदर वनमाली ।
27 संत दमोदर दयालदासू परमांनंद कै गुर बेसासू ।
चतुरदास मरदनिया नीकौं जगनाथ मोहन अरू टीकौं ।
28 तेजानंद रू माधौ भाषूं बासा रू सुषानंद कूं राषूं
बाई रमां रू चतुरा जोधौ जगनाथ परमांनंद सोधौ ।
29 चतुरा अरू भगवान दयालू रामदास सेवग गोपालू ।
सौ दोइ सै दिन के तहां बढही ज्यूं बरिषा रूति नदिया चढही ।
30 स्वामीजी कौ दरसन पावै जनम सुफल करि हरि गुन गावै ।
अंगसेवग स्वामी के कहे बहुत संत अनगिने रहे ।
31 प्रथम पयानै सांभरि आऐ देस देस के साधू धाऐ ।
दादूदीनदयाल की लीला निसदिन गाई ।
जनगोपाल जगदीस की भगति मुक्ति गति पाई ।

Fourteen

1 सांभरि सेवग महेसदासू गोइंद कै हरि कौ बेसासू ।
लालदास दमोदर षेमां नांदा फरहू सुंदर पेमां ।
2 दामोदर टीकूं गुरभाई हरीदास संत सुषदाई ।
सांभरि लीला आठौं नीकी सुंदर सेवग स्वांमीजी की ।
3 नगर नरांनैं बषनां ल्यायौ मिले संत बहु बिधि सुष पायौ ।
बषनां लीला नीकी कीनीं स्वामी रहे दूयौस तहां तीनीं ।
4 भरांणैं उधौ लै जाई लीला करी सु स्वामी भाई ।
अरू बचूंनि है मोहनदासू भाव भगति हरि कौ बेसासू ।
5 पून्यांनै तौल्हा लै जाई दूवारै लीला भली बनाई ।
आरति सहित आरती कीनीं स्वांमी ताहि भगति मति दीनीं ।
6 लघुगोपाल र टीला छीतर लै गयौ गाउ रतनपुर भीतर ।
बिधि सू कीये महोछे चारी अरू उधौ सेवग सुषकारी ।
7 रतनसुती रांनी राठौरी पुर पीपा र रांम की टौरी ।
कनकावती जु लैं न षदाई प्रोहिथ और दसौंधी आऐ ।

25B 4 सांचै BEF
26A 4 दूबरिया BEF ;B 1-2 कृष्नदास BEF
27A 4 रामदास BEF ;B 7 तीकौं BEF
30B 7 साध BEF

2A 2 तीकूं BEF
6B 7 ऊधौ BEF
7A 1 कनकसुता BEF
7B 6 प्रोहित BEF

8 और तीसरौ काइथ बैंनां हठु करि रांनी पठऐ लैंना ।
अति आनंदु भयौ आंबैरी सब ठां रांम दुहाई फेरी ।
9 भलौ महोछौ रांनीं कीनौं स्वांमीं ताकूं दरसन दीनौं ।
कपराचुपरा भेट मिठाई बांटि दइ आपु नहीं षाई ।
1 मोहन दफतरी सिरौंज जब आयौ भगति करी अरू भाव उपजायौ ।
सेवग भोजन ल्याऐ भारी मोहन उनकी प्रीति बिचारी ।
2 जे यहु भोजन स्वांमीं पावै तौ जीवन जनम सुफल है जावै ।
तब थाली आंबैरि पठाई स्वांमीं की चौकी परि आई ।
3 टीलै कह्यौ भोजन को ल्यायौ तब स्वामी मोहनदास बतायौ ।
जब स्वांमीं प्रचै भोग लगायौ तुरत थाल सिरौंज पहुचायौ ।
10 लालदास सेवग तहां माली जाकै भगति रीति की चाली ।
धारू रूपू परमांनंदू रामदास कै मनि आंनंदू ।
11 करांजली अनकहें जु आये तब रांनी सेवग दौराये ।
स्वांमीं तिनहीं दीयो संतोषू मानूं पायो जीवन मोषू ।
12 रामदास सेवग सुषदाई गुरपन राषै रांनी बाई ।
त्रिया पुरिष कौ नातौ मेट्यौ चरन कंवल बीरम तहां भेट्यौ ।
13 सांगानेर ले गऐ जु भेला हरि स्यूं प्रीति गुरू सूं मेला ।
हरीदास चाटसू वारौ उधौदास नरांयन सारौ ।
14 कारू कूंभा और नरांइंन सबही सेवग भगति परांइंन ।
सात महोछे नीके कीने कांनौंते कूं डेरा दीने ।
15 नीकौ नांती संगि नरांईन मन बच क्रम जगदीस परांईन ।
जनगोपाल के सिष संगाती चैंन भलौ दादू कौ नाती ।
16 भये उछाह चैंन कै भारी कियौ महोछौ श्रबसु वारी ।
रामदास मोहन अरू ऊधौ देईदास अरू लषनां सूधौ ।
17 तब स्वांमीं पगधारे सब संतनि के कारिज सारे ।
पहली लीला भई जु तीनी कांन्हांदास र बाई कीनीं ।
18 कुटी इकंति निजांम र नागर पगधारे धारे स्वांमीं सुषसागर ।
भाव भगति आरती कीनीं दरस पाई चरन रज लीनीं ।
1 अब छोडी अजमेरि की सिरदारी सो अब आये स्रणि तुम्हारी ।
उद्र निर्मति दुनियां मैं जांहीं तुम्ह बिन बिपति मेटै कोनांहीं ।
2 निजांम रू नागर बीनती यहु कीनीं तब स्वांमीं रजधांनीं दीनीं ।
पत्र ऊधौ करि सोई ज्यौ जब चाहौ तब भोजन लीज्यौ ।
19 जनगोपाल र जमुना बाई चौथी लीला तहां बनाई ।
सूरहरी टीकूं र दमोदर बाला हरि गुंनमांन सहोदर ।
20 पीपा ठाकुर और पिरागू दयालदास कै है बैरागू ।
चरणदास तहां रांका बंसी स्वांमी कौं सिष दिगमति गंसी ।

8B 6 ठांइ BEF
9A 7 अभैपद F
16B 1 हरीदास BEF
17A 2 स्वांमी बसई BEF
19B 2 तीकूं G

21 गांव टहटरा सेवग रांनां गांगा सांगा अरू भगवांनां ।
रांमदास अरू उधौ केसौ फुंनि द्यौसा मैं कीया पयेसौ ।
22 षेमदास सेवग अधिकारी भाई माधौ की मति सारी ।
बाल्क सबै रू सेवग छाजू मथुराबाई हरि काजू ।
23 और बोहरौ नराइन नीकौ अधिक उदार सूरिवांजी कौ ।
भगवांनीदास र माधौ पंडा भाव भगति कौ रोप्यौ झंडा ।
24 जगजीवन कै आऐ स्वांमीं नीकै रिझये अंतरजांमीं ।
लीला करी महोछौ भारी रहे डूंगरी पहरे चारी ।
25 हरीदास जंत्री बैरागी हरि गुन गावै यहु मति जागी ।
अरू भगवांनदास बैरागी संत संगति करि माया त्यागी ।
26 कल्यांणपाटण स्वांमी आये लाषा नरहरि कै मनि भाये ।
भाव भगति आरती बनाई लीला दोइ सरस करवाई ।
27 बहुत भांति पहरांवनि दींनीं ज्यूं षीवां र नराइन कींनीं ।
स्यामदास अरू हरिषांबाई हेमी बनमाली तुलसी सुषदाई ।
28 आंधो दामोदर अधिकाई भाव भगति करि प्रीति बढाई
लीला सरस महोछौ कीनौं सबही संतनि कौं सुष दीनौं ।
29 परबत बोहिथ पूरन भाई गरीबदास लीला करवाई ।
साल्हा षेमदास अरू केसौ द्यौराजहि पूरन उपदेसौ ।
30 चतुरा बिसनदास अरू ध्यांनां बाला कै सेवा कौ ग्यांनां ।
सब कौं सुष दे स्वांमीं चले थौहराई सेवग भले ।
31 सूरहरी दरसन तब पायौ रामहरी स्वांमीं तब आयौ ।
चतुरभुज रांमदत भाई षेमदास सेवग सुषदाई ।
32 भगति महोछे लीला नीकी अस्तुति कींनीं स्वांमींजी की ।
आग्या दे स्वांमीं पगधारे गांव रतनपुर तबहि सिधारे ।
33 माधौ रांमदास सुष पाये तब स्वांमी आगै चलि आये ।
मारग मांहि बसे दिन तीनी फुंनि सांभरि मैं लीला कींनीं ।
1 इक बैरागी मन मैं दोष उपजायौ स्वांमीं कौं मारण तहां आयौ ।
तब स्वांमी अचिरज इक कियौ अनूपा भास्यौ स्वांमीं उनकै रूपा
2 बैरागी कौं चेलौं मार मचाई तब स्वांमीं कहौ क्या कीयौ भाई ।
प्रताप तुमारौ सह्यौ न जाई ताथैं सजा इनौं यौं पाई ।
3 तब बैरागी मन मैं डरप्यौ भाइ चेलां सहत पर्‌यौ पग आई ।
हंम स्वांमीं अब सिष तुम्हारा बूडत राषौ प्रांण हमारा ।
4 दादू जाकूं मारण जाइये सोई फिरि मारै ।
जाकौं तारण जाइये सोई फिरि तारै ।
34 फुंनि कल्यांणपुर बैठे आई दीनदयाल सबनि सुषदाई ।

21B 3 ऊधौ BEF
22B 7 हरि सूं BEF
23A 2 बैहरौ G बहुरौ BEF
27A 7 दमोदर BEF;B 4-5 हरीदास BEF
29B 5 देवराज B
31A 5 राहौरी BEF

दादूदीनदयालजी दई सबनि कौं मौज ।
जंनगोपाल सूकै नहीं ज्यौं बरसै आसौज ।

Fifteen

1 चतुभुज नाइक कौ बेटा गुर दादू सूं भई जु भेटा ।
पूरब मैं परसिधि बषांनौं सेवग संत भये तें जांनौं ।
2 बौरीबारौ जैमल भाषूं किस्नदास संगति मैं राषूं ।
स्यांमदास कौ सिष प्रहिलादू पीपा राषै गुर मरजादू ।
3 कल्यांणदास जादू तेग्वारू षेता षरौ र पूरनसारू ।
रांमदास दामोदर मोटा दूदा हरि बीरम हरि की बोटा ।
4 लषिमीदास रू माधौ केसौ धरमदास कूं गुर उपदेसौ ।
स्वांमी कौ सेवग सब टांडौ गांव मोरडै लीला मांडौ ।
5 स्वांमीजी पधराऐ ज्ञाई बहुत भांति तिनि की बधाई ।
दरसन देषि सबनि सुष पायौ परमांनंद बिनोद बढायौ ।
6 आरति करत प्रेम अति भइयौ सब कौं देह बिसरजन भइयौ ।
नरनारी नाचै अरू गांवै परमेसुर सूं प्रीति बढांवै ।
1 अदभुत रचनां केसरि बरषैं प्रांणी जंत सकल मिलि हरषैं ।
गऊ बैल अर सब बणजारे जीवत मुकति भये ते सारे ।
2 गुण गाये लैर्लीन है स्वांमी करी जु सैल ।
सबद सुणत ही उधरे बणिजारे अरू बैल ।
7 तिनकौं सुष दे स्वांमीं आये बरस ऐक तहां रहे सु भाये ।
समौं गुनसठां आये जबही साहिब सैंन दई हैं तबही ।
8 साठै मैं छाड़यौ संसारू साहिब कै मंनि भयौ बिचारू ।
ज्यूं तुम्ह भावै त्यूं षुसी हम राजी इस बात ।
दादू के दिल सिदक सूं भावै दिन कूं रात ।
9 स्वांमी चलन आपनौं सूझ्यौ करि बिचार यहु आगम बूझ्यौ ।
मंन मैं स्वांमी ढूढ्यौ ठांऊं निकटि सरोवर नीकौ गांऊं ।
1 जब यहु स्वांमीं इछ्या कीन्हीं नराईणदास कौं हरि आग्या दीन्हीं ।
नगर नराणै ल्यावौ अबही दषण मैं तैं आयौ तबही ।
10 जगमाल कौं षंधार बषांनूं नराईनदास बडौ जांनूं ।
दषिन मांहि भाव उपजायौ दुजंनसाल कह्यौ सो भायौ ।
11 नगर नराईनै आये जबहीं स्वांमीजी पगधारे जबहीं ।
अमरा भाई लैंन षंदायौ स्वांमीजी कूं लै करि आयौ ।
12 राजा कै मंनि संक न आंनीं बिप्रनि कहीं सो बात न मांनीं ।
हंम तौ भाग बडे निधि पाई बुरी कहै ताहि रामु दुहाई ।
13 मिले नराईनदास रू स्वांमी मानूं प्रगटे अंतरजांमीं ।
कथा कीरतन गोष्टि कीनीं थोरे हीं मैं सब लषि लीनीं ।
14 बाहरि भीतरि ठाहर देषी नीकैं अस्थलि रहे बमेकी ।
1 जब स्वांमीं त्रिपोले आया प्रगट सेसि तब दरस दिषाया ।

6:1A 1 अदबुत BE
8C 4 सदिक B सदक E

सेसि सैनि करी तिहि ठांई तब स्वांमीं आसण मांड्यौ जांहीं ।
द्वारौ कीयौ ताल की तीरा पीछै बाग निकटि ही नीरा ।
2 तब दत गोरष प्रहलाद पधारे नांम कबीर चौरासी सिधि सारे ।
ब्रह्मगोष्टि करी सब राति अंतरध्यांन भये प्रभाति ।
3 तब टीलै अरज स्वांमी सौं करी गोष्टि राति कौंन संगि परी ।
आवत जात न देष्या कोई रात्यौ गोष्टि बहुत जु होई ।
4 तब स्वांमी ये संत बताये ब्रह्म सरूप साध सो आये ।
ब्रह्मतेज तिनमैं प्रकासै आये संत भयौ तम नासै ।
5 साध मिले तब हरि मिले सब सुष आनंद मूर ।
दादू संगति साध की रांम रह्या भरपूर ।
15 देस देस के साधू धाये गिरही अरू बैरागी आये ।
कीनीं टहल आपनी देहा हरि की प्रीति गुरु स्यूं नेहा ।
16 मास दूयौंस मैं घर है आऐ परमेसुर ईहि बिधि करवाये ।
टीला केसौ गोइंददास गोपाल नरहरि कै हरि बेसास ।
17 ऐसी ठौर अतिहूं चहिये स्वामी कह्यौ पहल क्यूं न रहिये ।
सब संतनि कौं आग्या दीनी तब स्वांमीं यहु लीला कीनी ।
18 तन पर येक अवस्था ठाटी मोह पासि सबहींन की काटी ।
1 गवन समौं नीयरौ जब आयौ सब संतनि कौं नांव दिठायौ ।
अथ गरीबदासजी का प्रसन ।
2 अंत समौं स्वांमी कौं सूझ्यौ तब गरीबदासि इक प्रस्न बूझ्यौ ।
तुम्ह तौ चाल अधर चलाई हिंदू तुरक की हदि उठाई ।
3 कासी काबा अर पैकंबर देवा हिंदू तुरक लगे इहि सेवा ।
तुम्ह दून्यौं की त्यागी राहा पीछैं क्यूं करि है नृबाहा ।
4 देह हमारी राषौ भाई जो चाहै सो ज्वाब कराई ।
तुम्ह जिनि जांनौं बासै येहा पंच तत की नांहीं देहा ।
5 जे तुम्हरै संसै है कोई हाथ फेरि देषौ अब सोई ।
देह हमारै है परि नांहीं ज्यूं द्रपन मैं दीसै छांही ।
6 सरीर मांहि जब फेर्या हाथ दीप लोइ ज्यूं दीसै गात ।
दिष्टि परे परि मुष्टि न आया हूवा अचिरज साध सबाया ।
7 स्वांमीं तुम्ह हौ आप दयाला सब जीवन कहौ रछिपाला ।
परि करामाति सौं दुनिया आवै भजन मांहि अंत्र पंडि जावै ।
8 तब स्वांमीं कह्यौ दीपक ईहां बरइ जो पूछै सो ऊतर करई ।
बाती तेल न चहिये कोई गैबी जोति अषंड सु होई ।
9 गरीबदास तब समझे मांहीं करामाति कौं लीजै नांहीं ।
करामाति सौं माया आवै प्रमेस्वर स्यौं अंत्र पंडि जावै ।
10 जब गरीबदास देष्यौ निहकांम तब स्वांमीं कह्यौ रिछक है रांम ।
यहु कुटी है हरि कै द्वारै भीड पडें संकट सब टारै ।
11 दादू राषी रांम परि अपणी आप संबाहि ।
दूजा को देषौं नहीं ज्यौं जांणैं त्यौं निरबाहि ।
12 अबिनासी कै आसिरै अजरावर की वोट ।

17A 5-10 हरि की आज्ञा सौं सो लहिये BEF

दादू सरणैं साध कै कदे न लागै चोट ।
13 जो निरगुण मत मैं रहसी भाई ताकी अबगति करै सहाई ।
इष्ट भिष्ट कौं ठाहर नांहीं समझि देषौ अपणैं मन मांहीं ।
14 संति बचन यहु स्वांमीं भाष्यौ गरीबदासि सो हिरदै राष्यौ ।
गरीबदासा यह मन मैं चीनीं स्वांमीं मरणि सु निरभै दीनीं ।
15 दादू जिन कूं राषै सांईयां मारि न सकै कोइ ।
बाल न बांका करि सकै जो जग बैरी होइ ।
16 गरीबदास प्रस्न फिरि बूझै स्वांमी तुमकौं आगम सूझै ।
सब संतनि कै मनि यह होई इहि ठां संत इसौ फिरि कोई ।
17 तब स्वांमीं सुषन कह्यौ इक सोई सो मैं बरस संत इक होई ।
फिरि स्वांमी इक साषि सुणाई पीछै हलचल हैगी भाई ।
18 जो इष्ट मांहि पग रोप्या जाई ताकी करसी रांम सहाई ।
नगर ढंढौरौ फेरियौ सब को मारण धाइ ।
जनगोपाल जन प्रहलाद की येकै रांम सहाइ ।
19 जो महाप्रलै भी कबहूं होई भगति हमारी जाइ न कोई ।
निरगुण भगति अबिनासी भाइ ब्रह्मा बिस्न महेसुर गाई ।
20 दादू जैसा अबिचल रांम हौ तैसी भगति अलेष ।
इन दून्यौं कीमति नही सहंस मुषा कहै सेष ।
21 पांणी पवन सु नां हुते नांहीं धरणि अकासा ।
चंद सूर भी थे नहीं तदि का दादूदास ।
22 पदमां पदम जु चौकडी इतनां दिन की देह ।
अब परमारथ कारनैं दादू प्रगटे येह ।
23 जा दिन कृतम नां हुता होते हट न पट ।
हुता कबीरा रांम जन जिनि देषे औघट घट ।
कृपा करि अर दरसन दीनौं करि असनांन र भोजन कीनौं ।
19 ता पीछै बैठे ऐकंता आग्या तीनि भई भगवंता ।
पहली आग्या आग्या भाषौ दूजी हूं आग्या पय राषौ ।
20 तीजी आग्या कैं संगि स्वांमी देह तजी मिलि अंतरजांमीं ।
संबत है 1660 जेठहि बदि जु गये दिन आठा ।
21 थावर पहरू चढ्यौ दिन जबही ढिग सेवग सुधि पाई तबही ।
गरीबदास अरू जंन मसकीनौं पीपा सौंधौ तिनकूं दीनौं ।
22 बडौ गोपाल नराइन ठाढौ दूरगा सेवग मन कौ गाढौ ।
दयालदास अरू रजब आयौ गवन समैं दरसनु तिनि पायौ ।
23 तब टीला कूं सोधौ दीनौं सब संतन मिलि यहु मत कीनौं ।
बिरह अगनि का दाग दे जीवत म्रित गोर ।
24 दादू पहली घर कीया आदि हमारी ठौर ।
सबहीं कै धीरज मंन मांही कोई बाहरि भीतरि जांनैं नांही ।
25 भौरांनै परबतु अधिकारी तहां पधरावौ इहै बिचारी ।

18B 1-2 साध बुलाये BEF
19B 8-9 ही प्रराष्यौ BEF
24A 1 सबहिन BE सबहनि F

दिन द्वै पहल पालकी आई केसरि चंदन सूं चरचाई ।
26 ज्यूं स्वांमी आग्या देई धरियौ परबत मांहि ।
करनहार करि लेईगा तुम्हकौं च्यंता नांहि ।
27 परबत मांहि सिषर अति भारी राष्यौ अस्थलु रांम संवारी ।
सौरि बिछाई पहरे बागौ बोटि पछेवरा संत सभागौ ।
27 चोवा चंदन चरचि अबीरा सेवग संत सबै मन धीरा ।
कीरतनु करि ते फिरि आये सुनि यहु बात संत पछिताये ।
29 त्राहि त्राहि भाषै सब कोई अैसी साध न पहमी होई ।
ज्यूं दीपक बिनु घर अंधियारौ ससि बिन रैनि मात बिन बारौ ।
30 जैसैं जल बिन तलफै मछा सरवर बिन हंस गाई बिन बछा ।
बहु बिधि करि संतनि दुष पायौ कलि कबीर हरि पास सिधायौ ।
31 देषनि कौ दुनियां सब धाई पहलैं गयौ सौरि तिनि पाई ।
सब कोउ सोधौ करि आयौ और कछू सैंधान न पायौ ।
1 अचिरज बात इक अैसी भई अनदृष्टि पालिकी होई तब गई ।
सेवग संत कहैं मिलि दोई अजब तमासा देष्या सोई ।
2 गुर दादू रू कबीर की काया भई कपूर ।
रजब अजब देषिया श्रगुन नृगुन नूर ।
3 जंबक क्या षाइ अगिनि क्या जालै माटी गडै सु कौंन ।
दादू मिले दयाल कौं ज्यूं पांणी मैं लौंन ।
4 दादू जब दिल मिली दयाल सौं तब अंत्र कुछ नांहि ।
ज्यौं पाला पांणी कूं मिल्या त्यौं हरिजन हरि मांहि ।
5 काया सूषिम करि मिलै अैसा कोई ऐक ।
दादू आत्म ले मिले अैसे बहुत अनेक ।
6 आकार भार छाया अरू बास साध कपूरै चार्यौं नास ।
अंजन पलटि निरंजन न होइ यहु गति बूझै बिरला कोइ ।
7 दादू देही ले र उडे कलि मैं हूवा साध बडे ।
भूला लोग न जांणौं भेव दादू भया निरंजन देव ।
32 कबीर की गति करता दीनी कांननि सुनी सु देषत कीनी ।
ब्रह्मां बिश्न महेसू सूर आऐ साध सिध सनमुष है आये ।
33 गण गंध्रप मिलि मंगल गाये भये सनाथु हु दरसंन पाये ।
सिव जु कहै चलिये कविलासा रहैं समीप सदा सुषवासा ।
34 ब्रह्मलोक ब्रह्मां जु बतावै महाप्रलै लूं काल न आवै ।
बिश्न कहै बैकुंठि पधारौ अंम्रित पांन करौ सुष सारौ ।
35 सिध लोक सब सिध बतावैं रिधि सिधि थाढी ताहि न भावैं ।

25B 5 चिंता BEF
26B 2 पिछेवरा BEF
28A 9 पुहमी BEF
29A 5 बंधही CG
31A 9 पालकी BEF
33A 8 सु BEF
34A 8 ठाढी BEF

हरि कौ दास कहूं नही राचै सूषिम मोटी माया बांचै ।
36 संतनि सूं मिलि हरि गुन गावै पारब्रह्म सूं मिलि सचु पावै ।
दादूदीनदयाल की गति गोपाल न जांन ।
प्रांन प्यंड जोतिहि मिले ज्यूं जल जलहि समांन ।

Sixteen

1 गरीबदास तब कीनी असी बरनी जाई न कहीनै कैसी ।
स्वांमीं पीछैं भली बिचारी ज्यूं की त्यूं ही राषी भारी ।
2 बहुत भांति सुरातनु कीनौं दसौं दिसा कौं दल तब दीनौं ।
साध सती सुर यौं सोहै कारिज करै अरू काटै मोहै ।
3 बंस पेड बंस ज्यूं होई चंदन बिडै सु चंदन सोई ।
ज्यूं सीहनि कैं उपजै सीहा साधिक होई सिध की लीहा ।
4 सुनि सुनि संत दसौं दिस धाये ज्यूं बरिषा बादल नभि छाये ।
दसौं दिसा डेरा तब कीनौं मांनूं साहि पयांनू दीनौं ।
5 उतरे आई ताल की तीरा गाऊं बाग घर बाहरि भीरा ।
बडे बडे संत पहल सब राषै रहते पहते पीछैं भाषे ।
6 सांगा जसा अरू पहराजु बोहिथ देवा हरि स्यूं काजु ।
षेमदासदयाल पीपा बनमाली जन बिश्न समीपा ।
7 गरीबदास सामंग्रो लीनीं षरौ उदार न गिनती कीनीं ।
चावर दारि कनिक घृत भाई मैदा बांड बहुत तहां आईं ।
8 येकनि कौ सीधौ लै दीजै येकनि कौं भोजन बहु कीजै ।
ठट्यौ महोछौ जेठी पुन्यौं मावस थैं मावस लै दून्यूं ।
9 मास दिवस लौं लीला कीनी संतनि कौं पहरावनी दीनी ।
जेते टूक महोछै आये घर पर का लेते ते लाये ।
10 आये बहुत ताइ फेरिनी के जे सुषदाई स्वांमीजी के ।
रांमदास बाघा रू नरांइन हरीदास हरि भगति परांइन ।
11 राति दिवस कीरतनु होई जैजैकार करै सब कोई ।
सब संतनि बस्तर सब दीनां तन परद नीर ही कोपींनां ।
12 जीरन पत्र चैत झरि जाई पावस रूति बौहुर्यौ हरियाई ।
गरीबदास ते सब पहराये घर बाहर के जेते आये ।
13 जने जने कूं दिये पिछौरा अपनें और नहीं कौ ब्यौरा ।
गरी छुहारी लांग मीठाई राति दिवस इक तार लुटाई ।
14 परमेसुर कौं असी आई ज्यूं षरची त्यूं बर्टी सवाइं ।
संचितु कछु न तबहि मंगायौ हरि च्यंतमणि मैं सब आयौ ।
15 अपने काज करै हरि आपै जन कु जस दे निहचल थापै ।
1 अपनै बिरद की हरि आपै कीनीं ।
गरीबदास कौं हरि सोभा दीनीं ।

9A 3 लग BEF
10A 4 फेनी BEF
14A 8 बधी BEF

आप अकेला सब करे औरू कै सिर देइ ।
दादू सोभा दास कूं अपनां नांव न लेइ ।
16 सब संतनि मिलि टीकौ दीनौं गुर कौ आसनु बैठक दीनौं ।
गरीबदास स्वांमी सन मांना सब संतनि कै युं परवांना ।
17 गावै सुनें बिचारै कोई रांम भगति अंतरगति होई ।
ग्यांनहीन कै उपजै ग्यानौ पारब्रह्म सौं लागै ध्यांनु ।
18 मुरिष सुनें त बिद्या पावै न्रिधन सुनें त चलि धनु आवै ।
जो कामना बिचारें कोई मनसा बाचा निहचै होई ।
19 संतु सुनें सो अति सुष पावै सुध बुध कूं भारी भावै ।
सुनें असंत होई दुष भारी हिरदै सुध होई बनवारी ।
20 हरि साधु निहचै करि गावै भक्ति मुक्ति प्रमार्थ पावै ।
साधू सबै रांम की देही जिनकै नांही और सनेही ।
21 संत सुषी सुष पावै रांमां षांन पांन पूरन सब कांमां ।
साध दुषाये हरि दुष पावै साधुनि पीछैं दूयौर्‌यौ आवै ।
22 जदपि सकल बियापी कहिये साधनि बिनां कहूं नहीं लहिये ।
रोम रोम गाई कै षीरा अस्थन बिनां न पावै नीरा ।
23 ब्रह्म गाई त्रीयलोक मैं साधू अस्थन पांन ।
मुष मारग अंम्रित झरै कत ढूढै दादू आंन ।
24 सातौं समंद दोति जौ कीजै सवा लाष मेर मसि दीजै ।
अठारह भार गहै कर लेष सुरति लिषै न लहै बमेकं ।
25 सब बसुधा कागद जौ कीजै साधू रांम न अंत दीजै ।
मैं जु कहे अपनैं उनमांनैं भलौ बुरौ कोउ जिन मांनैं ।
26 बारह बरस बालापन गये गुर भेटे तै सनमुष भये ।
सांभरि आये समये तीसा गरीबदास जनमें बतीसा ।
27 मिले बयाला अकबर साही कल्यांणपुर पचासैं जांहीं ।
समैं गुन सठा नगर नरांइनैं साठै स्वांमी रांम समांनैं ।
28 सतगुर दादूदीनदयाल जति महाजन जनगोपाल ।
भाग बडै गुर सरनैं आयौ संत सिरोमनि कौ जसु गायौ ।
29 दादूदीनदयाल कौ बडौ महोछौ गाई ।
गरीबदास भक्ति दिढ जनगोपाल बलि जाई ।
इती श्री जन्म प्रजंत लीला संम्पूर्ण समाप्त ॥।

19A 11 उपावै BEF
19B 7-9 मलीन नहीं ज्ञान बिचारी BEF
24B 10 बमेकूं BE बमेकै F
28A 4 ज्ञाति BEF

CHAPTER 4

Concordance

In the desert of *nirguṇ bhakti* literature not all forms one encounters are found in the existing dictionaries. I publish here the first product of my efforts (and of the computer) to provide complete concordances of texts, as part of a Concordance of *bhakti* literature in several volumes, which should appear soon.

This grew out of the frustration I experience frequently: you have a form not found elsewhere in your text and, in that spelling, often not found in dictionaries. The form is attested by all manuscripts, but in the context the meaning is not clear. If more Kwic (Keyword in Context) Indexes were available, I could check the meaning in parallel passages elsewhere. The present Concordance is a start to meet this need.

The purpose of a complete Concordance is to make available to scholars all morphological forms that were current around 1600 AD. This should be a help for the translator of literature where such forms occur. For meanings I refer to the translation in Chapter 2. When, in the translation, a footnote has been added about the (obscure) meaning of a form, I mark the reference number in the Concordance with an asterisk (*).

An effort has been made to make visible (whenever orthographically possible) the relation between words, by using indentation and/or by separating the verbal roots. Considering the 'easy search' of a form to be a priority, I have respected the alphabetical order. In consequence, you may find related roots and forms on different places.

It is interesting to note that many words are found *only* in Manuscripts BEF which give the enlarged version. This can be seen from the definition string: e.g. 8;19;2.

The following words occur frequently in Jan Gopāl's narrative and they have been left out of the Concordance.

अब और कबीर करि करी करै कहा कह्यौ
का की कूं के कैं कोई कौं कौ
जाइ जु जो ज्यूं
तुम थैं दादू
नहीं नही नांहीं नांही बहुत बात
भगति भै माता यहु
रांम राजा सु सुष सेवग सो स्वांमीं
है

अ

आ

ऐ

क

छ

झ

ट

थ

फ

ब

ल

स

Bibliography

an., *Tukārām, Gāthā*, 2 vols, Bombay, Government Central Press, 1950.

T.H. Avaṭe, ed., *Sakal sant gāthā*, Poona, 1924.

V.S. Bhatnāgar, *Life and Times of Sawāi Jai Singh, (1688-1743)*, Delhi, 1974.

W.M. Callewaert:1973, 'Search for Manuscripts of the Dādūpanthī Literature in Rājasthān', in *Orientalia Lovaniensia Periodica*, 4,1973, 155-167.

W.M. Callewaert:1977, 'Search for Manuscripts of the Dādūpanthī Literature in Rājasthān,II', in *Orientalia Lovaniensia Periodica*, 8,1977, 305-308.

W.M. Callewaert:1978, *The Sarvāṅgī of the Dādūpanthī Rajab*, Leuven, 1978, 446p.

W.M. Callewaert:1980, with L. De Brabandere, 'Nirguṇ Literature on Microfilm in Leuven, Belgium', in *IAVRI Bulletin*, IX (Dec. 1981), 24-28.

P. Caturvedī, ed., *Dādūdayāl Granthāvalī*, NPS, Vārāṇasī, 1966

K.C. Jain, *Ancient Cities and Towns of Rājasthān*, Delhi, 1972.

A. Nāhaṭā, *Rāghavdāskrit Bhaktamāl*, Jodhpur, 1965.

W.G. Orr, *A Sixteenth-century Indian Mystic*, London, Lutterworth Press, 1947.

S.A. Rizvi, *A History of Sufism in India*, I, 1978. G.N. Śarmā, *Social Life in Medieval Rajasthan, (1500-1800)*, Agra, 1968.

P.H. Śarmā, *Sundar-Granthāvalī*, 2 vols., Calcutta, 1936.

V. Śarmā, *Sant-kavi Dādū aur unkā pantha*, New Delhi, 1969.

D. Shea and A. Troyer, eds., *Dabistān-i-mazāhib*, 3 vols. (Paris, 1843).

G.R. Siddons, 'Extract and Translation of one of the Granthas, or sacred Books, of the Dādūpanthī Sect,2' in *Journal of the Asiatic Society of Bengal* 6 (1837), pp. 481-87 and pp. 751-56.

K.P. Simha, *Dādūpantha evam uske sāhitya kā samikṣātmak adhyayan*, Vārāṇasī, 1971.

V. Smith:1966, *Akbar. The Great Mogul, 1542-1605*, (Oxford, 1917), New Delhi, 1966.

Sukh Dayāl Dādū, *Śrī Dādū Janma Līlā Parcī*, Jaipur, 1947.

Sv. Nārāyaṇ Dās, *Rāghav Dāskrit Bhaktamāl*, Pushkar, 1969.

Sv. Nārāyaṇ Dās, *Śrī Dādū charitāmrita*, 2 vols, Pushkar, 1975.

Sv. Nārāyaṇ Dās, *Śrī Dādū panth parichay*, Pushkar, 1979, 3 vols.

Monika Thiel-Horstmann:1983, *Crossing the Ocean of Existence, (Braj Bh. religious poetry from Rājasthān)*, Wiesbaden, 1983.

Monika Thiel-Horstmann:1983b, *Bhakti in Current Research*, 1979-1982, Berlin, 1983.

P.N. Tivārī, *Kabīr Granthāvalī*, Allahabad, 1961.

Ch. Vaudeville:1969 *L'Invocation. Le Haripāṭh de Dnyāndev*, Paris, 1969.

Ch. Vaudeville:1974 *Kabīr* I, Oxford, 1974.

H.H. Wilson, 'A Sketch of the *Religious Sects of the Hindus*', in *Asiatic Researches*, 16 (1828), pp.79ff.